future

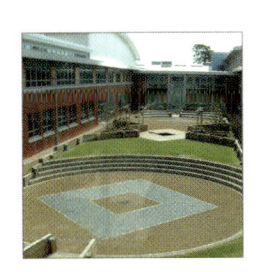

designing
school grounds

London: TSO

TSO

Published by TSO (The Stationery Office) and available from:

Online
www.tsoshop.co.uk

Mail, Telephone, Fax & E-mail
TSO
PO Box 29, Norwich, NR3 1GN
Telephone orders/General enquiries: 0870 600 5522
Fax orders: 0870 600 5533
E-mail: customer.services@tso.co.uk
Textphone 0870 240 3701

TSO Shops
123 Kingsway, London, WC2B 6PQ
020 7242 6393 Fax 020 7242 6394
16 Arthur Street, Belfast BT1 4GD
028 9023 8451 Fax 028 9023 5401
71 Lothian Road, Edinburgh EH3 9AZ
0870 606 5566 Fax 0870 606 5588

TSO@Blackwell and other Accredited Agents

Published with the permission of the Department for Education and Skills on behalf of the Controller of Her Majesty's Stationery Office

© Crown copyright 2006

Copyright in the typographical arrangement and design rests with the Crown.

This publication, excluding the Royal Arms and any logos, may be reproduced free of charge in any format or medium for research, private study or for internal circulation within an organisation. This is subject to it being reproduced accurately and not used in a misleading context. The material must be acknowledged as Crown copyright and the title of the publication specified.

This is a value added publication which falls outside the scope of the HMSO Class Licence.

Applications for reproduction should be made in writing to
HMSO, The Licensing Division, St Clements House, 2-16 Colegate, Norwich NR3 1BQ
Fax: 01603 72300 or e-mail: copyright@hmso.gov.uk

ISBN-13: 978 0 11 271182 7
ISBN-10: 0 11 271182 0

Printed in the United Kingdom for The Stationery Office
N5430712 09/06 C10 348361

foreword

I am very pleased to be introducing this guide. School grounds are potentially as important to the education and overall well-being of our children as are school buildings, and they are often an under-used and under-regarded asset. This guide encourages schools to consider how best to use their grounds for the educational, recreational and social needs of their pupils. It gives encouraging practical case studies of where schools have transformed their environment and brought new learning and excitement for their children, staff and the wider community.

Capital funding for all schools has risen sharply over the past few years, and we are currently in an unprecedented period of opportunity and large-scale investment in education from which all schools can benefit. Every school gets substantial money each year for its own investment needs, and further money goes to authorities who prioritise it to school needs. In addition, two key programmes are aimed at modernising schools for the needs of the 21st century:

- **Building Schools for the Future** (BSF) – remodelling or renewing all secondary schools in England in 15 waves of investment starting in 2005-06, and;
- the **Primary Capital Strategy** – additional capital investment, starting with £150 million in 2008-09 and rising to £500 million by 2009-10, to support a programme to renew at least half of all primary schools over the next 15 years or so.

This is a wonderful opportunity to improve school grounds as well as school buildings. 63% of the whole schools estate is land rather than buildings, but often the potential of the school grounds is not fully considered and developed. The 2005 House of Commons Education and Skills Committee report, 'Education Outside the Classroom' concluded that *"school grounds are a vital resource for learning"* and that… *"capital projects [should] devote as much attention to the 'outdoor classroom' as to the innovative design of buildings and indoor space"*. When imaginatively developed, school grounds can contribute to curriculum teaching and learning, and to better recreational and social interaction of their pupils. As well as contributing strongly to children's understanding of 'green' issues, they can make a positive impact on the sustainability of the schools and their locality. They can also encourage children to take part in a range of physical activities, which contribute so much to their health and well-being.

Integrated thinking and design are crucial to the successful development of schools' buildings and outside spaces to achieve these aims. This design guide shows, through a number of live examples, how well-designed, well-used and well-maintained school grounds can provide a wonderful resource that can benefit staff, pupils and the wider community.

The DfES is pleased to have worked in partnership with Learning through Landscapes on this publication and very much appreciates the work they continue to do particularly the support they provide to schools to help them make the most of their school grounds.

Jim Knight, Minister of State for Schools and 14-19 Learners

Department for Education and Skills

Contents

about this guide	**4**
Who is it for?	4
How it works	5
introduction	**7**
section one: developing school grounds – the process	**11**
Common issues and considerations	12
Developing existing school grounds	20
Developing grounds for new schools	30
Case study: Leesland Infant School, Gosport	38
section two: designing and building	**45**
Common design issues	46
Designing and building for… learning and teaching	54
An alternative teaching space	54
Specialist features	60
Experiential learning	62
Designing and building for… healthy lifestyles	64
Physical activity and active play	64
Emotional well-being	67
Growing food	68
Safety, risk and challenge	70
Designing and building for… positive behaviour	72
Reducing opportunities for conflict	72
Developing environments conducive to social interaction	74
Reducing damage and opportunities for theft	76
Surveillance, supervision and 'capable guardians'	76
Designing and building for… community use and development	78
Safe child-focused environment	78
Focus for community action	78
A centrally-valued community resource	80
Designing and building for… sustainable outcomes	84
Sustainable design and management	84
Conserving and enhancing nature	86
Experimenting with innovative sustainable techniques	87
Working together and belonging	88
Embedding	89
Designing and building for… different sectors and needs	90
Early years	90
Primary	93
Secondary	94
Special Educational Needs	96
section three: supporting school grounds development	**99**
Who can help?	100
Funding	105
Accessing funds	108
section four: further information	**111**
Glossary of terms	112
Text references and information sources	115
Further reading	117

◀ **Left**
Mulgrave Primary
School, Greenwich

about this guide

This guide is full of information, guidance and ideas to inspire the best possible designs for school grounds, as well as examples of schools that have used the development of their grounds to enhance the formal, informal and hidden curricula.

Who is it for?

It's for everyone involved in developing school grounds – teachers, headteachers and governing bodies, local authorities, architects, dioceses and sponsors. It's particularly relevant to people who make decisions about capital and revenue spending, want to increase the educational opportunities offered by schools, or are involved in designing school sites.

Considering all users at the outset will ensure the grounds benefit the wider community.

For pupils and staff

The most successful and sustainable school grounds projects fully involve staff and pupils from across the school. As the real clients of any improvements to the school grounds, pupils and staff need to have an active role in the development of their outdoor spaces – from surveying what already exists and how people feel about it, through the development and implementation of the strategic (or master) plan, to the ongoing development, management and use of the space. By taking part, pupils and staff have a sense of ownership and empowerment.

For headteachers, governing bodies and those providing extended services

Headteachers and governing bodies have clear visions for their school's future, in terms both of teaching and ethos. Well-designed and -managed school grounds have a key role to play in their achievement – major building works are an opportunity to enhance and realise the school's vision, particularly with an integrated approach to designing the indoor and outdoor spaces. But many improvements can be achieved without large-scale, high-cost developments. This guide has guidance and examples from all points on the investment scale.

For local authorities and dioceses

The local authority (LA) can play a vital role in school grounds development, particularly in the context of new-build schools. The LA ensures that each school addresses the needs highlighted in the Asset Management Plan (AMP), as well as wider local strategies in areas such as inclusion, current or future specialisms, leisure and sports provision and other extended schools facilities. Well-designed, -used and -managed school grounds have the potential to contribute to LA improvement targets set out in a range of strategies, including those for biodiversity, transport, and crime and disorder. The LA can provide specialist advice and support on aspects such as design and health and safety.

For landscape architects, architects and other building professionals

Integrated thinking is fundamental to good design, build, use and management of schools, with the indoor and outdoor spaces treated as a continuum. Designers and contractors have specific skills that can complement those of educationalists, and a collaborative approach to school grounds design can bring outstanding results. Their expertise can ensure high-quality design, which will make a real difference to learning and children's experiences. There will be increasing opportunities for teams to develop their educational expertise, as well as consultative and participative skills. This is especially true for medium-sized and smaller firms, which can contribute local knowledge and experience to enhance their communities.

How it works

This guide has been designed so that users can dip into the sections that interest them, rather than necessarily reading from start to finish.

- It considers all school sectors – early years, primary, secondary and Special Educational Needs – looking at the development of existing spaces as well as new build and remodelled schools, and including individual perspectives of each sector.

- Examples from recent school grounds development projects are used to highlight ideas to consider in designing and building outside spaces for schools.

- Although the use and management of school grounds are not discussed in detail, they are critical to the long-term success of school grounds and something you will need to think about at all stages of the design process.

- It's not a technical guide – the reference section signposts you to further, specific information.

There are four main sections, outlined in the box on the right.

section one: Developing school grounds – the process

Guidance on the process of creating or improving school grounds, divided into three parts:

- **Issues common to existing and new-build sites**: preparing the brief, design quality indicators and participation
- **Developing existing school grounds**: a four-step process of change, which can be applied to existing sites and communities
- **Developing grounds for new schools**: different kinds of sites, the design process as it applies to new sites

section two: Designing and building

How school grounds can benefit staff, pupils and the wider community, and how to design to maximise that benefit. This section introduces common design issues, and is then organised by themes:

- **Learning and teaching**: the formal, informal and hidden curricula, including play
- **Healthy lifestyles**: exercise, emotional well-being and growing food; balancing safety, risk and challenge
- **Positive behaviour**: how design can influence behaviour
- **Community use and development**: the role of schools as a focus for community activity
- **Sustainable outcomes**: how school grounds design can embrace sustainability and provide opportunities for understanding
- **Different sectors**: specific considerations for early years, primary, secondary and special school pupils

section three: Supporting school grounds development

- **Who can help**: where to go for practical help and advice
- **Funding**: sources of available funding and how to access them, including developing a fund-raising strategy

section four: Further information

- Glossary
- **Text references and information sources**: reference details, publications, websites and organisations providing information

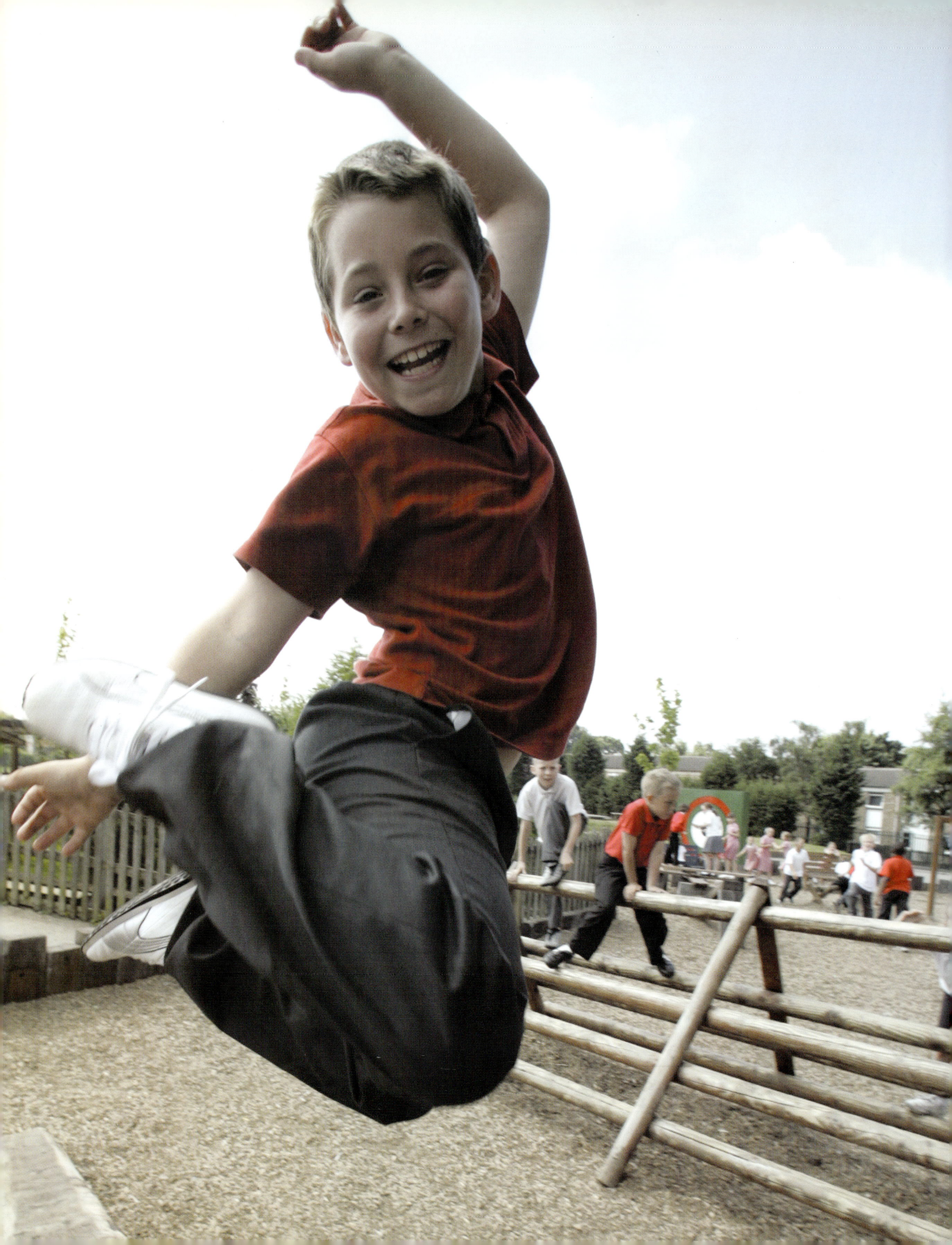

introduction

The importance of school grounds

The framework document *Every Child Matters*[2] aims to ensure that every child and young person has the opportunity to fulfil their potential.

It identifies five overarching outcomes that all Government departments with a vested interest in children's development should be working towards. These are:

- be healthy
- be safe
- enjoy and achieve
- make a positive contribution
- achieve economic well-being.

School grounds can play a significant role in delivering these outcomes, providing safe, stimulating environments where children and young people can learn, explore, play and grow, regardless of their educational needs.

As a society, we recognise that our young people are being offered ever fewer opportunities for safe, challenging, active and collaborative play. Lack of these opportunities can lead to health issues, apathy, social and behavioural issues. School grounds can help raise achievement and self-esteem, improve behaviour and health, and help children and young people develop a wide range of skills.

◀ **Left**
Coleshill Heath Primary School, Solihull

School grounds can be designed, built and developed over time to enrich teaching and learning across the whole curriculum. Children's learning can be enhanced outside – they find lessons outdoors more relaxed, interesting and easier to understand, and they think their teachers are "friendlier outdoors". Teachers report that the grounds provide access to resources not available in a classroom and opportunities to use different teaching styles. Making more use of school grounds can also foster stronger relationships between staff and pupils, and between pupils themselves, leading to significant improvements in behaviour, attitudes to learning and attainment levels.

As well as playing a crucial role in delivering the formal curriculum, including much of PE, school grounds should be designed to address both the informal curriculum (social use of the grounds at breaktime and during the extended day) and the hidden curriculum (the messages and meanings children receive indirectly). The grounds provide wonderful opportunities for children and young people to take an active part in developing and managing their school environment. Through simple outdoor improvement projects they can learn new skills, understand the value of team-working, assess needs, make decisions on priorities and manage projects.

School grounds that are interesting and safe will encourage secondary-age pupils to stay on site at break times. Sheltered or semi-sheltered areas can be used as eating areas, when the weather allows, to promote the take-up of healthy school meals.

School grounds are also a national environmental resource, integral to the delivery of many of a local authority's wider environmental and social strategies. They provide opportunities for children not only to implement elements of these strategies, but also to learn about key issues and re-connect with the natural environment.

Integrated thinking and design

A whole-school approach is essential to the design and development of school buildings and grounds. Simple ideas such as linking dining areas with the outdoor space, bearing in mind supervision, can increase flexibility and make spaces more enjoyable to use; factoring in vehicle access and pupil movement patterns at different times of day can make the space safer and more effective.

Schools and local authorities should look holistically at capital funding, considering the whole site and not just the buildings. Working closely with professional experts, they need to embrace a philosophy of organic growth within an often rigid design and build process, supporting the continued and phased development of the grounds in the medium- and long-term.

Working together

Educationalists and children should be fully involved in the design process, actively participating both in the creation (or transformation) and the maintenance of their learning environment. Architects, landscape architects and support professionals must become hands-on facilitators and leaders of thoughtful and relevant change – or must work with those who are and can.

This can be more problematic than using a prescriptive process for design and build but the results from involving pupils can be wonderful and provide real benefits to the school.

POND/WATER FEATURE

BOG

section **one**

**developing
school grounds
– the process**

Common issues and considerations

School grounds have historically been the last aspect of school design to be thought of and the first element to be cut when budgets are strained.

But they can have a dramatic impact on improving learning, promoting positive behaviour, encouraging better concentration in lessons and developing a healthier generation through a variety of active play.

The design process depends on a number of factors, particularly whether existing or new-build school grounds are being developed. Some basic principles apply to both. This section looks at the common issues and then concentrates specifically on the two situations.

The whole school site

The development of the school buildings and grounds should always be planned together – even building refurbishment schemes can provide opportunities to add or rationalise outdoor spaces. In practice it's often the building that takes priority but designing the school before fully understanding the site and what it has to offer can lead to inefficiencies in the design process and compromises in the layout as well as in future sustainable use and maintenance.

There are differences between developing buildings and developing school grounds:

- Whereas building requirements are usually clearly set down in detail, the brief for the grounds seldom extends beyond a page or two of generic aspirations. Indeed, for a grounds project at an existing school, there may be no formal brief at all.

- School buildings need to be complete on the day of opening, whereas in order to get the most out of the school grounds it's important to leave opportunities for development by the school.

- The grounds are a dynamic environment which will change over time to respond to the needs of the school and its community. They must provide flexible opportunities for ongoing formal and informal curricular use. In this way the changing needs and character of the school community can be accommodated, maintaining the school as a living part of the community it serves.

Preparing the brief

It's worth spending time developing a strong external brief. If the local authority has developed a planning brief for the site, this can often be a good starting point for site layout.

▶ **Right**
This multi-functional space, with easy access from each end, includes an amphitheatre as an outdoor teaching and performance space, and a solar-powered fountain – a teaching and aesthetic feature.

▶▶ **Far right**
A disused swimming pool and changing rooms transformed into an indoor teaching/performance space, linked to the main school building by an outdoor amphitheatre.

Points to consider:

- A school grounds brief should be developed by a landscape architect in conjunction with parents, pupils and staff at the school.

- Pupils working with adults to make decisions about their grounds witness citizenship in action. Young people gain a sense of belonging and understand the roles they can play in the wider community.

- Briefing should happen in conjunction with local planning officers and, where possible, involve local community councils and community groups.

- The brief needs to include the objectives of the design against which a scheme can be tested. The objectives on the right are a useful model for an outdoor space brief.

- For most projects it is usually appropriate to have a performance brief – but for PFI schemes it's advisable to add specific lists of what is to be provided in the school grounds. The external space is in effect a large classroom and therefore should be given the same level of detail in its specification.

LANDSCAPE OBJECTIVES

- Create a landscape setting suitable for school and community

- Meet educational and social needs

- Provide a safe, diverse and stimulating environment

- Accommodate a range of activities/opportunities

- Build in flexibility to accommodate change/development

- Design buildings and grounds as one entity

- Balance design, management and use against aesthetic, functional and financial considerations

- Ensure environmental fit

- Incorporate sustainability within the design, eg for surface water treatment, and cut and fill where physically possible

EDUCATIONAL OBJECTIVES

- Allow children to participate

- Provide outdoor teaching spaces that are sheltered, safe and secure

- Lay out space and facilities for all forms of play

- Stimulate creativity

- Contribute to pupils' health and well-being

- Create places where nature may thrive

- Celebrate diversity

- Encourage responsibility through citizenship

- Provide opportunities for enriching the curriculum

- Provide sports facilities of a suitable standard

- Be located at the heart of the community

section one: developing school grounds – the process

▶ creativity…

▶ diversity…

Design Quality Indicators

The Design Quality Indicator (DQI) for Schools[3] can be used at the briefing stage to help raise aspirations and manage expectations of all stakeholder groups involved in the project (see box opposite).

Project management

The most successful school grounds development projects are led by a steering group with specific devolved roles and responsibilities.

- This helps to ensure that the project meets the needs of the users, is sustainable in the longer term, and makes best use of all available skills and experience.

- The make-up of this group depends on a number of factors:
  - whether the project is part of a new-build or an existing site
  - the project scope
  - the time and resources available.

- The group may include pupils, teaching and other school staff, community members (such as parents), governors and design or school grounds professionals, each involved to a greater or lesser degree at different stages.

14 designing school grounds

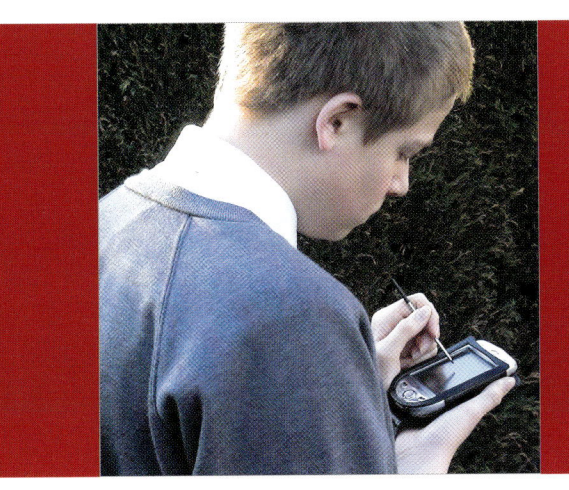

▶ curriculum… ▶ health and well-being…

DQI FOR SCHOOLS

The schools version of the Design Quality Indicator (DQI) differs from the Construction Industry Council's (CIC) generic DQI in that it uses language that's more tailored to school users and introduces attributes of the building and school grounds that are specific to schools:

- At mid-design stage, it's used to check how the design is progressing, and to measure against the original aspirations.
- When the building has been completed for a year or more, it's used as a post-occupancy evaluation tool. The information gathered at this stage informs the client and the design team about how the building and school grounds are performing and can be fed back into the briefing stage for the next project.

The DQI for Schools can also be used as part of an ongoing evaluation for the buildings and grounds in the longer term. This is particularly important for the outside space, which needs to evolve over a longer period of time to ensure it realises its full potential and continues to meet the needs of the school.

The questionnaires ask respondents to focus on three separate aspects of school grounds design:

- Is there adequate space to allow for all the functions required for good school grounds, both now and in the future?

- Does the design of the grounds provide for the whole of the formal and informal curriculum?

- Do the grounds meet basic requirements for children's health, safety and welfare while still being stimulating?

The DQI for Schools is intended for use at all three stages on Building Schools for the Future projects from Wave 2 onwards, and its use will be encouraged on all other schools projects costing £1m or more. But as a design, monitoring and evaluation tool for outside spaces, the DQI for Schools can be applied to any school grounds development, both for existing spaces and new sites.

www.dqi.org.uk/schools

◀ **Left**
Working with a landscape architect is a valuable experience for children allowing them to question or even challenge ideas.

▼ **Below**
In this entrance, pupils helped create a memory wall comprising past and present student-named bricks and resin memory blocks.

Consultation and participation

The needs of all stakeholders using the outside space – pupils, teachers, other school staff and the local community – should be fundamental to its design. And knowing when to involve them is crucial to the success of the project. They should be fully consulted at all stages of the process, not only to clarify needs but also to identify solutions. School grounds designed without full understanding of these users' needs won't maximise their potential and will often be found wanting. It's also important to think about the ongoing use and management of the site.[4]

There are various approaches to encouraging stakeholders to take part, depending on the circumstances of each school. See pages 20-27 for more details.

Participation can be through the taught curriculum or through extra-curricular structures such as school councils. The latter approach can help to support the development of participatory skills among staff and pupils – it fits very closely with Citizenship initiatives. The curriculum-based model supports developments within particular curriculum subjects and their associated teaching and learning practices, but it does require some flexibility around curriculum planning. Further information and guidance is available from Learning through Landscapes.

The learning opportunities that participation provides help to ensure that changes made truly meet the needs of the school – and it means that all pupils feel a sense of inclusion. It also engenders a sense of ownership, which wouldn't occur if a solution were imposed upon them – and it makes children more likely to respect their environment.

Actively involving pupils can improve their self-confidence as well as developing subject-specific and wider skills. For example:

- **PSHE and Citizenship** – skills of consultation, collaboration, problem solving and decision making are central to school grounds projects. *"Most importantly the students learned they can work as a team. A lot of kids don't like teamwork – there's too much rivalry."* Secondary teacher. Working together on a shared project leads to closer relationships between children and adults. *"As soon as we were given the opportunity to talk to each other we realised we all wanted the same thing. Teachers and pupils started discussing the ways forward and how to make decisions and plans."* Primary pupil.

- **Design and Technology** – practical experience of designing and making skills. One school grounds project carried out through the Design and Technology curriculum, helped students gain *"an understanding of the things that happen when you design things, as well as first-hand experience of time scheduling, seeing machines, learning about industrial safety and planning"*. Head of Design and Technology.

- **Vocational and applied courses in secondary schools** – the grounds can be used to provide a real context for students and at the same time bring about improvements such as environmental features, seating areas or gardens that benefit the whole school.

Pupil participation

Pupils can participate in a number of ways. At this primary school Year 6 pupils created mood boards as inspiration for their new garden. They then created their own designs, which were displayed. Questionnaire cards were designed for feedback, and elements of all the designs were incorporated into a formal design. A range of school policies supported the development.

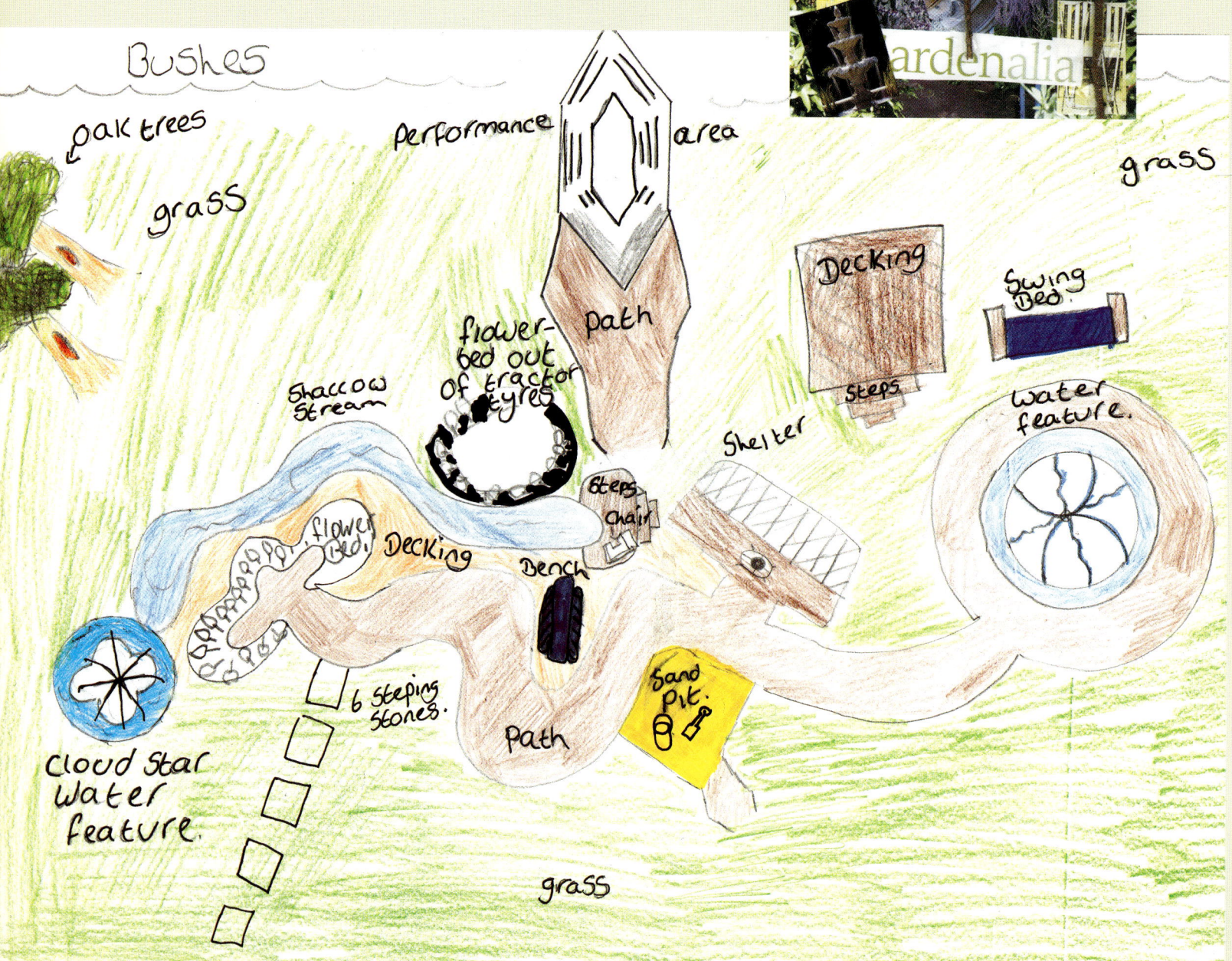

18 designing school grounds

section one: developing school grounds – the process   19

▶ **Right**
Pupils can carry out much of the information gathering on all aspects of the site.

Developing existing school grounds

Planning to make changes

There are many ways of approaching school grounds development at an existing school – by implementing a long-term school development or strategy plan for the site in stages, for example; using available funds to make small improvements across the whole site; or concentrating on one area in order to make a big impact – which may well inspire further efforts.

Whatever the approach, improvements should be made within the framework of a whole-site strategy plan. This will help to ensure that any changes are sustainable and don't create future conflict of use.

There are different models of the design process but all include surveying the site, researching needs, designing changes, and implementation. This is summarised in the diagram opposite[5] which illustrates the Learning through Landscapes process of change.

Where are we now?

Key information to be collected at this stage includes:

What physical features are in the school grounds now?

As well as a physical survey of the site, you need to gather information on legal, technical and financial or policy issues that may affect the changes you want to make. For example, you need to confirm who owns the land, whether there are any restrictions on its use, who is responsible for maintenance, and where services such as electricity, gas, water or telephones are located above and below ground.

How do we use the grounds now?

What activities take place in the grounds before school, during break and lunchtimes and after school? How do different groups use the grounds and how do they influence each other? How are the grounds managed? Who uses the grounds out of school hours?

How do we feel about the grounds?

By asking people to think about the physical aspects of the grounds and how they use them, you're encouraging them to think about how they feel about them. What kinds of emotional response do people have, both positive and negative?

All members of the school community will have valuable insights into how the grounds are used. There are various ways of collecting information from different groups – it's very important to devise an approach that will work for the school. Information gathering can be done gradually, perhaps through lessons or after-school clubs, or be concentrated into a short period to maintain momentum and keep interest levels high.

The Learning through Landscapes process of change

By the end of this stage you should have a vision plan showing what you would like to achieve; how you would like your grounds to function; and how you would like to be able to use them.

By the end of this stage you should have a good knowledge of: the existing layout and features of your school grounds; how the grounds are maintained and whether they are in good condition; how the grounds are used and viewed by the whole school community; and any technical and legal constraints that exist.

Where do we want to be?
- What would we like to be able to do in the school grounds?
- Developing a vision for our school grounds

Where are we now?
- What do we have?
- How do we use the grounds?
- How do we feel about the grounds?

Involvement

Communication

Funding

Maintenance

How can we get there?
- Solving problems
- Developing detailed design

Making the changes
- Implementing plans
- Celebrating our achievements
- Maintaining our new grounds
- Using the new facilities

By the end of this stage you should have detailed plans for the immediate changes you hope to make. You should also have considered the maintenance implications.

A step-by-step action plan setting out targets and responsibilities will help keep your project on track.

By the end of this stage you should have improved your grounds, and be ready to think about future projects.

◀ Left
A courtyard space for redevelopment, and pupils' ideas.

▼▶ Below and right
Children and young people have lots of ideas about their grounds and how they would like them to be used.

Where do we want to be?

To guide the development, it's crucial to identify what it needs to achieve, such as:

- enhancing teaching and learning by creating new facilities and inspirational learning environments
- providing for the needs of all children, including those with SEN and disability
- improving how pupils and staff feel about their daily workplace
- creating learning opportunities for pupils throughout the process of change
- making the school site more welcoming and accessible for the local community.

Asking "What do we want to do in the grounds?" or "How would we like to use the grounds?" rather than "What would we like to have?" will focus discussion on the real needs of the school rather than generating a 'wish list' of features.

This consultation can result in a vision plan that will:

- define the shape and sizes of the different spaces
- identify existing or potential uses, users and possible improvements
- indicate major features, for example large areas of planting, main routes through and access points
- give an overview, with the flexibility to evolve over time.

It's often at this stage that schools turn to professional designers to help them develop their plans.

Rebecca would like pencils to climb on and to sit on and to bounce upon. If you sit on the pencils you might get spiked!

designing school grounds

Lily would like a wooden play house in the outside area

David would really love a wooden climbing frame in the outside area.

sycamore
apple tree
Tog wall
woodchip path
holly
Dogrose
Wildflower meadow
Pond
flower beds
bird house
hide
Dog
mini beasts area
Path

Pupil participation

Children at this primary school wanted to create a small garden to highlight the signpost. They decided to plant butterfly-friendly plants, making the garden butterfly shaped. They came up with a range of designs, looking at symmetrical patterns.

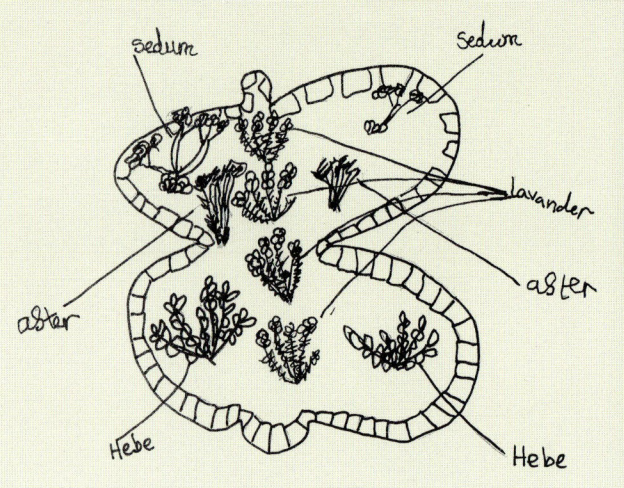

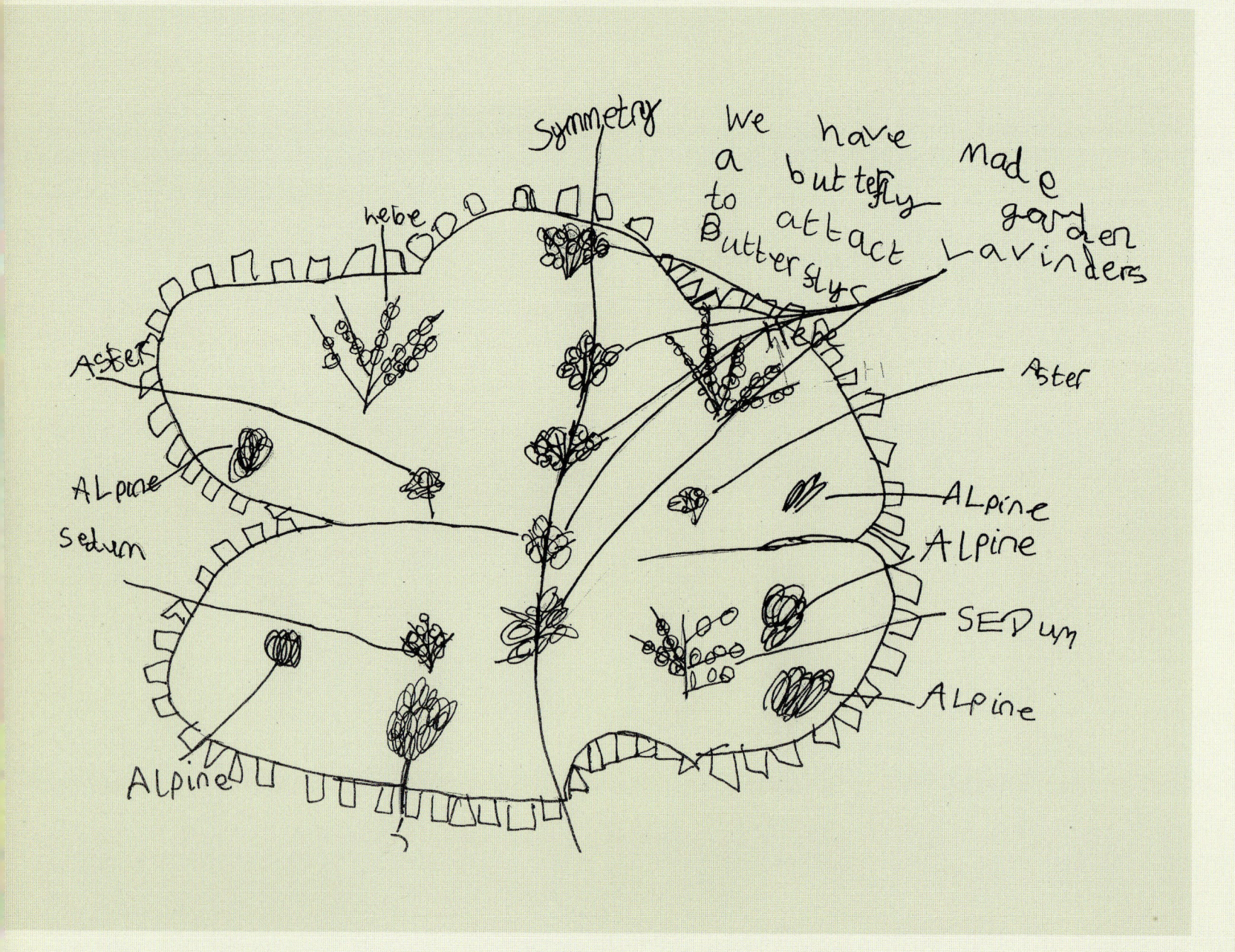

24 designing school grounds

▶ **Right**
Pupils enjoy being involved in the construction work.

How can we get there?

For every need identified there may be several solutions. As well as physical improvements, changes may also need to be made to the management and maintenance of the site, along with specialist training for teachers and supervisory staff. Changes that can be made without major physical upheaval or large funding implications can often bring rich rewards in the early stages of a project.

Once the areas for development have been identified, they need to be explored in more detail, either all together, or in phases, taking into account:

- cost
- space requirements
- materials and where to get them
- how to build/create the feature
- who might help
- how the new spaces will be used and maintained in the long-term[6].

The **further information** section gives potential sources of information for these details.

section one: developing school grounds – the process 25

Pupil participation

Older children worked with the younger ones to help develop plans for their playground at this primary school. Staff, parents, governors and the local community were also invited to feed in ideas. To create a new climbing structure, children visited an outdoor centre for ideas, and then created images and models before the final structure was built.

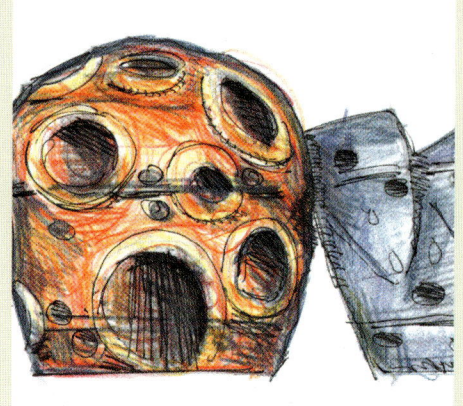

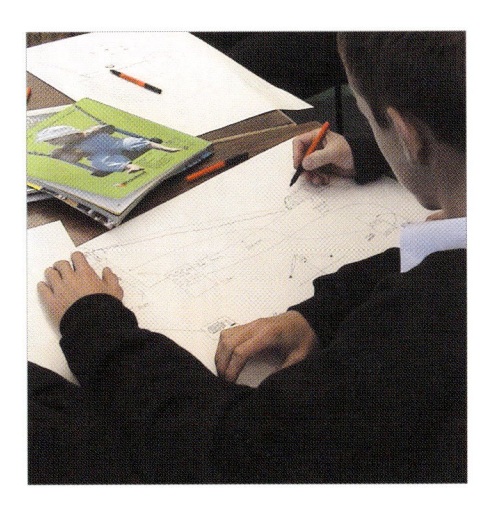

◀ **Left**
Secondary technology students worked with professional playground designers to design bespoke seating and activity equipment for the grounds.

"To keep children's enthusiasm, the project needs to be plan-build-plan-build-plan-build so that they can see something growing and developing… You need an interim physical reality so the kids have faith that something's going to happen."

Deputy Headteacher, Hampshire

Making it happen

Pupils, parents or other volunteers are often keen to help create features. A skills audit will help to identify the resources available and ensure that you can make judicious use of the professionals involved. Some of the work may not be suitable for active involvement of children but it's still important to keep them informed, perhaps by watching and recording work in progress, or inviting contractors to come and talk about the project.

It may also be necessary to involve contractors – either as part of an existing relationship, or by bringing in specialists.

What happens afterwards?

The work doesn't stop once the improvements have been carried out:

- **Celebrate** – tell the media, have a launch event, recognise the achievements of the pupils involved, show your gratitude to everyone who helped with the project.
- **Maintain the new grounds** – make sure that the project will continue to be successful in the long term.
- **Use the new facilities** – do staff need training to help them make the most of the outdoor environment?
- **Evaluate** – how well have the objectives been met? Reflect on what has been learned. In other words, ask again…

Where are we now?

It's unlikely that the grounds are now perfect – and they certainly won't stay perfect for ever. School grounds improvements should be a continuous cycle to ensure that they will suit the needs of future generations of pupils.

"Our school grounds project has tangibly increased pride in the school environment and been responsible for an enduring feel-good factor. It has raised expectations and been the catalyst for an avalanche of ideas and inspirational projects for self-help improvement. The spin-off effects on learning for marginal students has been massive, and committed students became even more committed."

Headteacher, Devon

Developing an existing space

Pupils at this junior school worked with an artist-in-residence to develop their magical sensory garden, an area full of artwork, scents, texture, colour and gentle sounds. After consultation, priorities were agreed and all children in the school participated in at least one aspect of the garden at all stages of the project. They were able to record their thoughts and ideas in a communal ideas and progress book.

▶ **Right**
After watching the wildlife the pupils created their own birdbaths from scrap.

▼ **Below**
The spiral trough will be planted with a range of sensory plants.

▶▶ **Far right**
An area was created for temporary art.

◀ **Below right**
The children worked in small groups to paint the mural.

28 designing school grounds

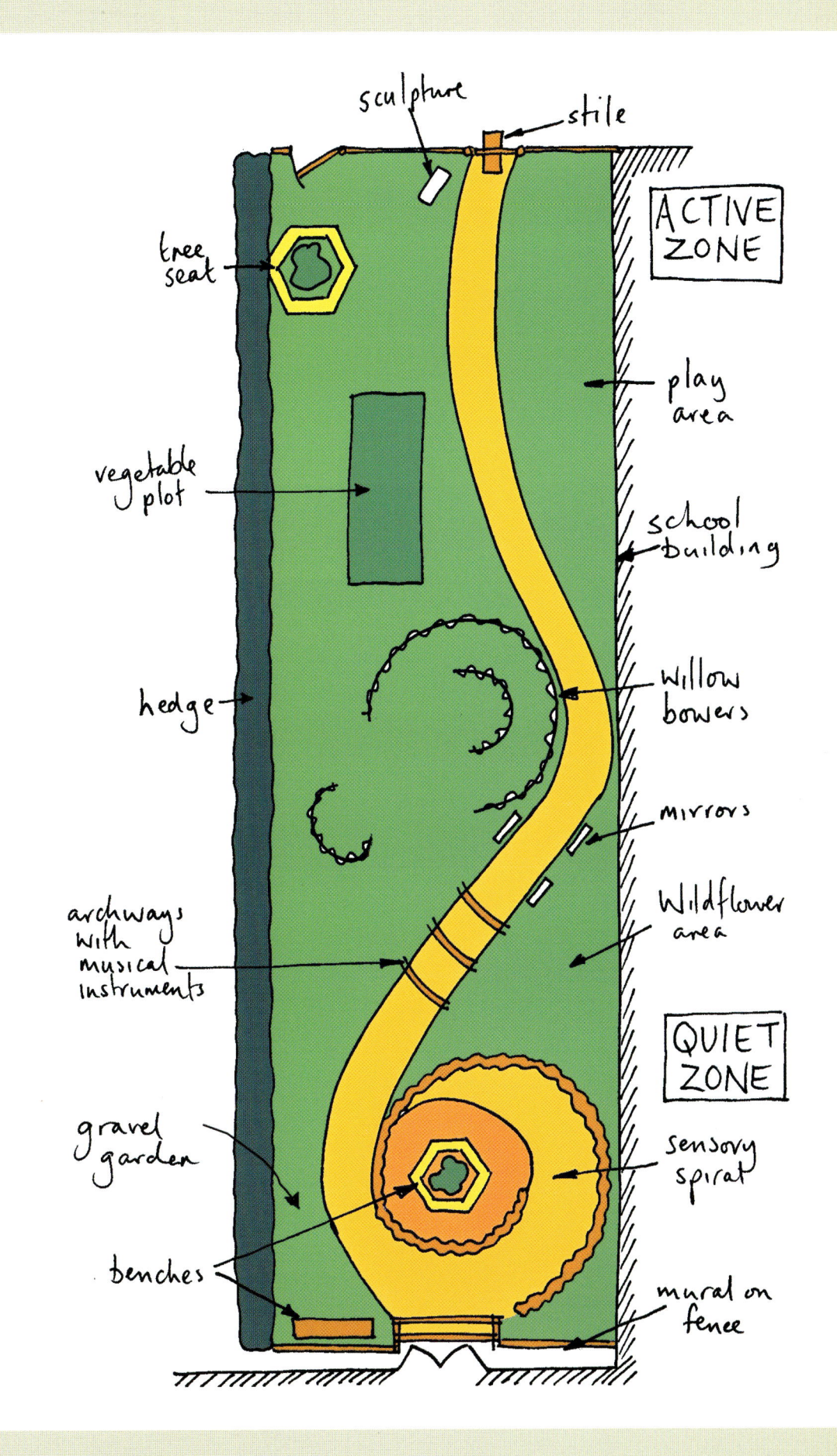

section one: developing school grounds – the process   29

Developing grounds for new schools

A key difference between new and existing schools is the make up of the school communities and how they can take part in the school grounds development process.

You can read more about the process of preparation and implementation in a school capital project in the Making It Happen chapter of *Transforming Schools: an inspirational guide to remodelling secondary schools.*[7]

Choosing sites
Brownfield sites

Schools often need to be redeveloped on their existing site because of urban constraints and community requirements – but there are advantages to this:

- The existing school population and the surrounding community are already familiar with the location and how to access it.

- Planning restrictions are usually less onerous than on a greenfield site.

- Existing roads and services may not need much upgrading if the school roll remains constant.

- It may be possible to retain elements of school grounds already developed by the school, along with the 'sense of place' they provide. This option is often available to merging schools, in which case a special effort should be made to ensure the school can embrace its new identity.

The main difficulty with developing an existing site is that the school must continue to function during the construction of the new buildings and grounds.

Points to consider:

- Access for pupils and staff

- Fire assembly areas and pick-up and drop-off points, which may be part of the construction site

- Maintenance of utilities serving the school

- Long diversions to create safe distance from new construction areas

- If existing sports pitches have to be built on, the topsoil should be stored in accordance with BS4498 to protect the soil structure for future use. Poor soil structure is the largest contributory factor towards playing fields being out of use. Decanting during the development process offers advantages over the tandem build, freeing up the master planning process.

▶ **Right**
A new school's courtyard became an integral, safe play area animated with sculptures.

◀ **Below**
This well-used courtyard is at the centre of new and existing buildings.

▶▶ **Far right**
Improving an existing courtyard was part of a whole-school remodelling project.

Greenfield sites

The challenge in building new schools on greenfield sites is to ensure that the school is at the heart of the community. Greenfield sites are usually either publicly owned land, such as parks, or land at the edge of a community where new housing development is either restricted or encouraged.

Points to consider:

- Think about the needs of the wider community and potential opportunities for enhanced facilities.
- If new housing is being encouraged, the school grounds design must ensure that access arrangements are flexible enough to account for this.
- Schools sited next to new housing often need additional planting to enhance the boundary, which can affect available play space.
- It's worth negotiating whether any such buffer zones can be developed for access as additional learning or play space.

section one: developing school grounds – the process   31

Merging schools

A primary school in Devon had developed very successful school grounds over a number of years before they joined another on a new site. The staff and pupils at both schools wanted to ensure that the new grounds were just as well designed and used, and that all pupils had an opportunity to make their mark. Pupils were consulted on what they liked and valued about their old grounds, and which elements they would like incorporated into the new. This was done in a number of ways with all year groups.

◣ **Below left**
Pupils were asked to draw what they would like to see through the windows of their new school.

▼ **Below**
Pupils were asked to vote on their favourite areas of the grounds. The response from each year group was recorded separately.

🟩 Foundation stage
🟥 Year 2
🟦 Year 3

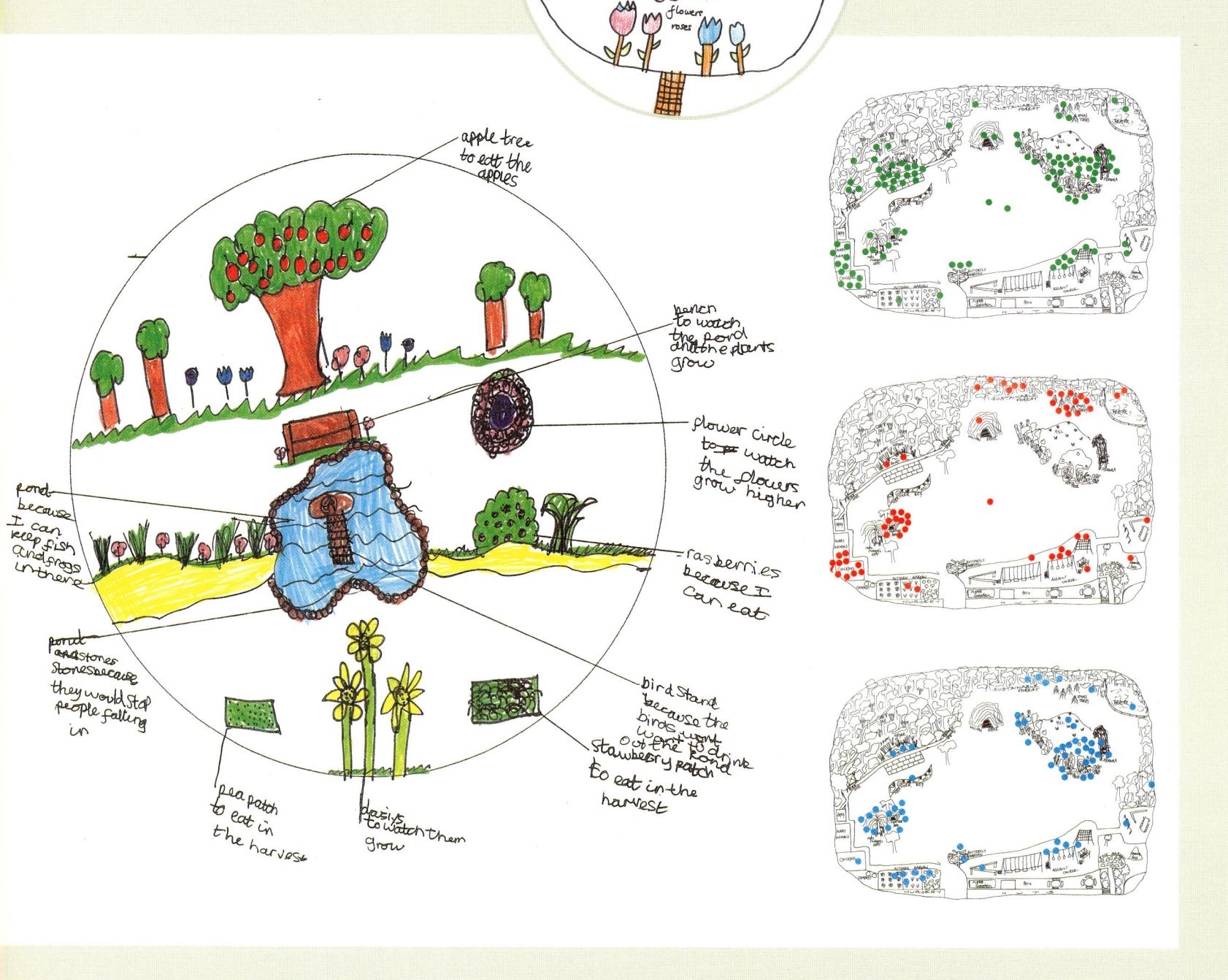

32 designing school grounds

Consultation and participation for new-build schools

Although it's more difficult than in existing schools, the need to consult and participate with the existing or new school communities is just as critical. How this is achieved depends on individual circumstances – and each situation is unique.

Points to consider:

- A brand new school built from scratch means that there may be no school community in place, although a headteacher or chair of governors may have been appointed. Consultation can still take place with appointed individuals, community groups and future pupils.

- The holistic approach is just as important – it's vital that the whole site be considered from an educational as well as a landscape point of view (see OBJECTIVES on page 13) as this may affect the orientation and location of the buildings and spaces within the site.

- The space designed should be flexible, allowing for future development by the incoming school community.

Merging schools

Where two separate schools or two parts of a school are being merged onto a single site, the new school grounds can be a way of keeping the best of each and helping to forge a new, strong, single identity.

Points to consider:

- Cultural aspects of the two communities can be represented on the new site through the selection of plants, the designs of paving, or the creation of details on fences and panels that can be used throughout the site.

- Staff and pupils could start identifying these at their existing sites at the early stages of planning the new school.

- Both communities need to be involved on an equal footing to identify any new needs that the site will be expected to meet and to ensure that these are factored into any landscape and building planning.

- The merger of different age schools, such as infant and junior, will involve slightly different issues from the merger of similar-age schools.

- Outdoor provision needs to be of similar quality and, if possible, quantity, whether older children are moving to the younger site, or vice versa. This will avoid resentment and ensure that all pupils have a sense of place and safety.

- The new school will need to create its own unique identity and the grounds should provide a space in which to do this.

- It helps to identify and protect a budget that the new headteacher can use to develop the grounds.

Landscape architects

As part of a PFI bid for a new learning community, landscape architects provided proposals for new facilities to include a children's centre, primary and secondary schools, and a special school, along with community learning, arts and sports facilities.

◤ Below left
A whole-site plan sets the design in context and illustrates the seamless integration of the building and landscape.

◤ Bottom left
The proposed building fits within the sloping topography and creates interlinked spaces for multiple uses.

▼ Below
Each outside classroom has an individual, secure, outdoor space with hard area and lawn. Soft landscaping and planting provide enclosure and opportunities for sensory experiences.

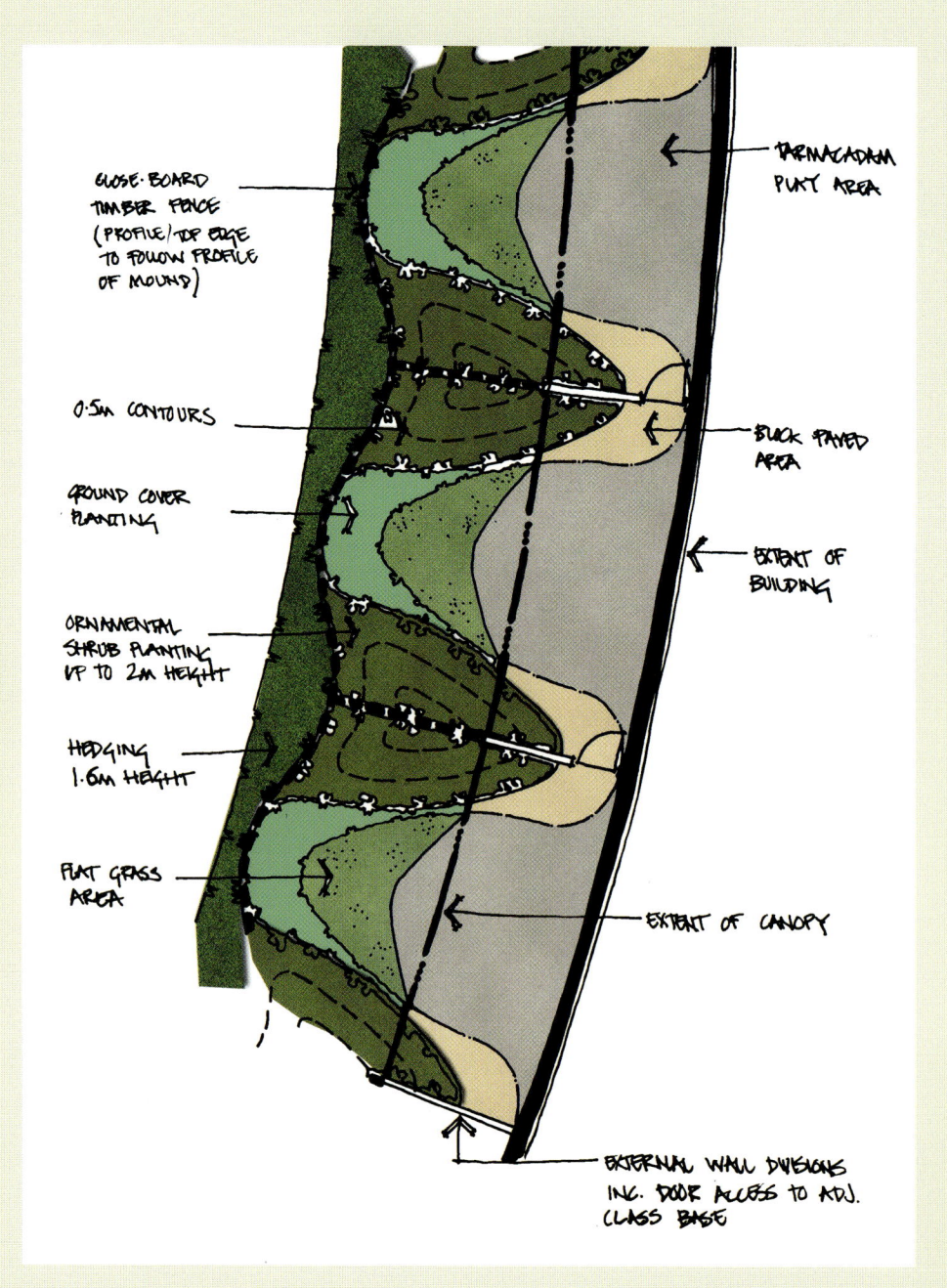

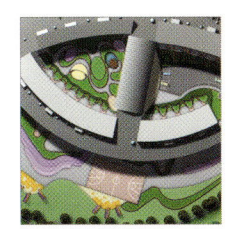

The design process for new build school sites

Developing the school grounds is a complex process and requires a team of integrated skills – it's important that the interplay between architect, landscape architect and engineer is fluid and that everyone has a clear understanding of their roles and responsibilities.

Points to consider:

- Cost
- Space requirements
- Materials and where to get them
- How to build/create the feature
- Who might help
- How the feature will be used and maintained in the long term.

Read more about relevant issues in the **designing and building** section.

Site investigation

- The site investigation should be carried out in accordance with BS5930, which clearly sets out the detail required.
- Physical site opportunities and constraints, linked with planning and transportation requirements, will form the basis of the initial zoning diagram.
- Educational needs and building layout opportunities overlaid on the site will further crystallise the masterplan or strategy plan.
- At an early stage it's advisable to check title plans for the site. Whilst the local authority may own adjacent land, easements need to be understood prior to detail design.

Analysing needs

A full understanding of the landscape and educational needs is crucial before the site structure can be worked out. The **designing and building** section of this guide outlines some of the key themes that should be considered.

Developing site structure

- The site structure will be largely defined by buildings and routes.
- You will need to know exactly how the outside space will be used and its relationship to the buildings before starting to develop the site structure.
- It's also worth considering a site security plan.

◀ **Left**
Access to buildings should also be considered. Wide doors and a gentle slope ensure quick and easy access for all staff and pupils.

SPORTS FACILITIES

Playing fields can be particularly difficult to locate on a site because of their size.

Points to consider:

- The range and frequency of PE and sports activities.

- The balance between grass and synthetic pitches – on heavy soil the cost of providing grass pitches can outweigh the benefit, so a synthetic pitch may be the better option.

- If you're considering all-weather pitches, you need to understand the sports to be played – this can affect the type of surface material specified.

- Don't miss the opportunity to provide for summer sports – jump pits and throwing circles are economical considering the benefit they can offer. And if you can provide a double football pitch, a full range of athletics can also be accommodated. A synthetic cricket wicket between the pitches will add another sport opportunity to the curriculum without much call for additional space.

- It may be appropriate to make provision for after-hours users by including floodlighting to increase the time they can be available. (This would be subject to planning permission and would need a costed ongoing management plan to cover the additional use of the site.)

There's further information in the DfES publication *Inspirational Design for PE and Sport Spaces*.[8]

Roads and access

Roads and access requirements can take up a large amount of the site, reducing available play, sports and learning space.

Points to consider:

- A rigorous Green Travel Plan can significantly reduce the most area-hungry needs of pupil pick-up and drop-off.

- Designing bus drop-off areas that can be closed to vehicles through the school day can allow for additional playground space during this time and additional parking for community activities in the evening.

- There may need to be off-site road works to bring adjacent roads up to standard to accommodate the school traffic and to slow traffic down outside the school gates.

- Even the smallest changes of level across the site have repercussions in the design of exterior spaces.
- As a general rule, you should provide for emergency access paths, allowing access to one third of the perimeter of the school building.
- Cherry picker access also needs to be provided for windows and gutters to be maintained. This needn't be traditional hard surface – reinforced grass will suffice.

Planting

Once a landscape structure has been decided upon, long-term structural planting can be considered. With a good landscape structure, change within the site can be dynamic and ongoing, creating contrasting spaces of varying sizes and qualities, to suit different users.

Points to consider:

- Long-term planting needs to be done before building work starts to give the site the added benefit of several months' growing time while the building work takes place.
- Structural planting can provide:
  - a softer, more defined edge to the perimeter
  - a shelter belt to reduce heating costs
  - a sound barrier to reduce road noise
  - hedges and/or trees to break up windswept playing fields and establish a sense of landscape appropriate to young people.

AT A GLANCE

- Integrate the design of buildings and grounds
- Consider both landscape and educational objectives within a brief
- Use DQIs for development and evaluation
- Tailor the design process to suit the school community for long-term success
- Plan for and encourage full participation of the existing or new school community
- Make sure formal, informal and hidden curricular needs are met
- Ensure the adaptability of the outdoor space – and design for its continued development and evolution
- Allocate finance to the medium- and long-term development of the outside space
- Plan for the use, management and maintenance of the site and spaces
- Consider access and security of the site
- Make sure there's a strong site structure

The support and resources to draw upon will depend upon what stage the new-build is at. There's further information in the **who can help?** and reference sections.

section one: developing school grounds – the process

Leesland Infant School worked in partnership with a landscape architect, adopting a process which proved very effective in managing changes to the site.

This case study illustrates some of the process principles covered in **section one** of this book, along with some of the themes that schools need to consider in the design and use of their grounds (see **section two**).

"The process was invaluable as we gained a thorough understanding of the whole site and the needs of the children before developing our ideas with expert guidance."

Jane McDowell, Headteacher

Case study:
Leesland Infant School, Gosport

The new main gate

Quiet/imaginative play area

Leesland Infant School has 250 pupils and is in a small, restricted site in a residential, urban area. The site is dominated by a large red brick Victorian building. To the front was an all tarmac playground, to the back an early years area, and to the side a staff/visitor car park and a further tarmac area designated as a 'no go' area for pupils.

When the school decided it was time to make improvements to its outdoor space it focused initially on the development of a single area. After discussions with other schools who advocated a whole-site integrated approach, it embarked on a process of consultation, planning, designing and construction. A strategy for the grounds was developed in partnership with a dedicated local authority team, the Hampshire Schools Landscape Programme (HSLP), before the school moved on to make changes within their grounds. HSLP use a detailed planning and designing process, which can be seen on the opposite page. A landscape architect from the team worked closely with the school throughout the process.

The process

Leesland Infant School was guided through a well-established set of steps to help ensure the school grounds development was completed in a thorough and sustainable way.

This process is described further in the **developing school grounds** section.

1 Information gathering (Activities)
2 Feedback (Residency)
3 Evaluation (Document)
4 Exploring options (Zoning activities)
5 Whole site planning and design
5 Grounds strategy document
6 Identifying projects (Action planning and prioritising)
7 Engaging others (Design/project briefs)
8 Developing detail (Design/management /use plans)
9 Making change (Construction /management)
8 Implementing change
10 Using and managing (Monitoring)
11 Reviewing (Annual/five year)

The staff car park before it was converted

Where are we now?

By the end of this stage the school wanted to have a thorough understanding of:

- the existing layout and features of the grounds
- the condition and suitability of the current provision
- any technical or legal constraints.

The school set up a working party involving representatives from across the school community, especially the children, and set about gathering information about the existing site issues. Two spaces were identified as having particular problems: the playground and the car park.

The playground:

- a tarmac-covered space with limited play opportunities, favouring more boisterous types of play
- on a cold, windy part of the site
- next to a noisy main road and relatively busy public footpath
- separated from public areas by railings only
- overshadowed by an imposing Victorian building, out of scale with infant children.

The staff car park:

- stopping the use of a set of double doors out of the hall due to health and safety concerns
- bounded by a relatively recent single-storey extension used by the reception classes with a key entrance into the car park not used because of health and safety concerns
- used by parents, pupils and siblings to access the early years classrooms
- in a warm, sheltered spot next to a quiet traffic-free lane.

case study: Leesland Infant School   39

Amphitheatre/assembly space

PE and active play area

Quiet/imaginative play area

Where do we want to be?

By the end of this stage the school wanted a vision plan showing:

- what it would like to achieve
- how the grounds should function
- how the spaces would relate to each other and be used.

A whole range of groups, including the children, representing all aspects of the school's different functions, worked to produce a set of summaries outlining what they would like to be able to do in their grounds and how the different spaces would function.

A landscape architect from HSLP worked for several days alongside representatives from the whole school community to gather feedback from these consultations. HSLP then produced an evaluation report and, working in partnership with the school, used this information to develop a whole-site strategy.

A whole-site strategy

Developed in partnership with the school and HSLP, the whole-site strategy identified the need to explore opportunities for:

- Relocating the car park to the neighbouring junior school or elsewhere on the site
- Redesigning the released, sheltered area to provide:
  - a play space to include opportunities for imaginative and quiet play
  - a teaching space that would exploit the links with the hall
  - an outdoor area for events, assemblies, outdoor eating and waiting parents
  - a safe access route to early years classrooms
- Utilising the 'no go' area, made safe by new arrangements, for play
- Redefining use of the existing front play space for boisterous, active play and games.

Key:

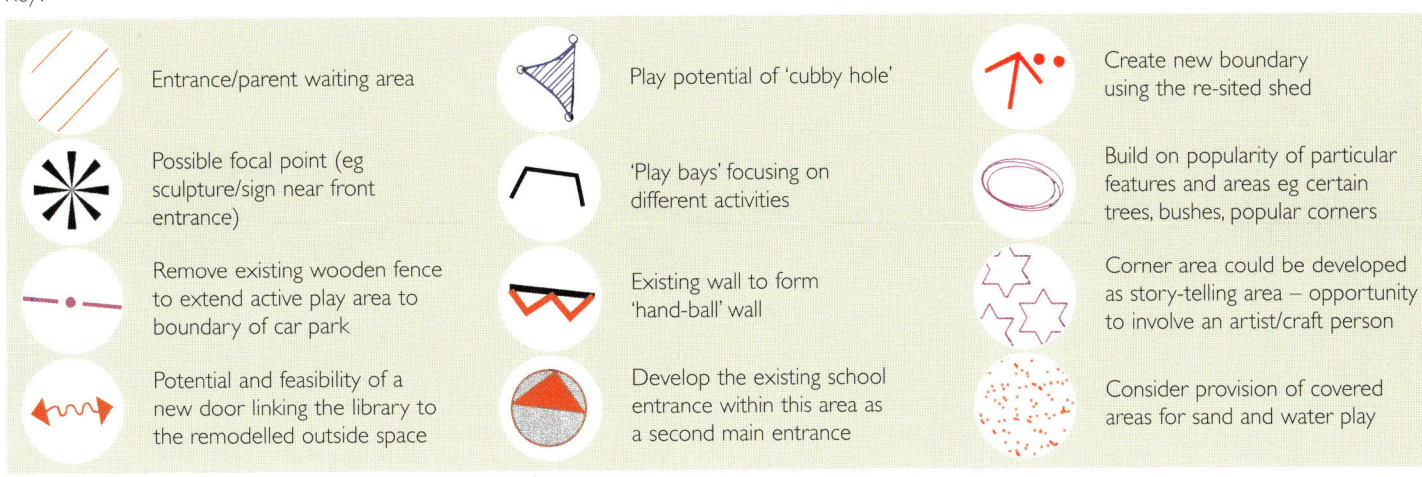

- Entrance/parent waiting area
- Possible focal point (eg sculpture/sign near front entrance)
- Remove existing wooden fence to extend active play area to boundary of car park
- Potential and feasibility of a new door linking the library to the remodelled outside space
- Play potential of 'cubby hole'
- 'Play bays' focusing on different activities
- Existing wall to form 'hand-ball' wall
- Develop the existing school entrance within this area as a second main entrance
- Create new boundary using the re-sited shed
- Build on popularity of particular features and areas eg certain trees, bushes, popular corners
- Corner area could be developed as story-telling area – opportunity to involve an artist/craft person
- Consider provision of covered areas for sand and water play

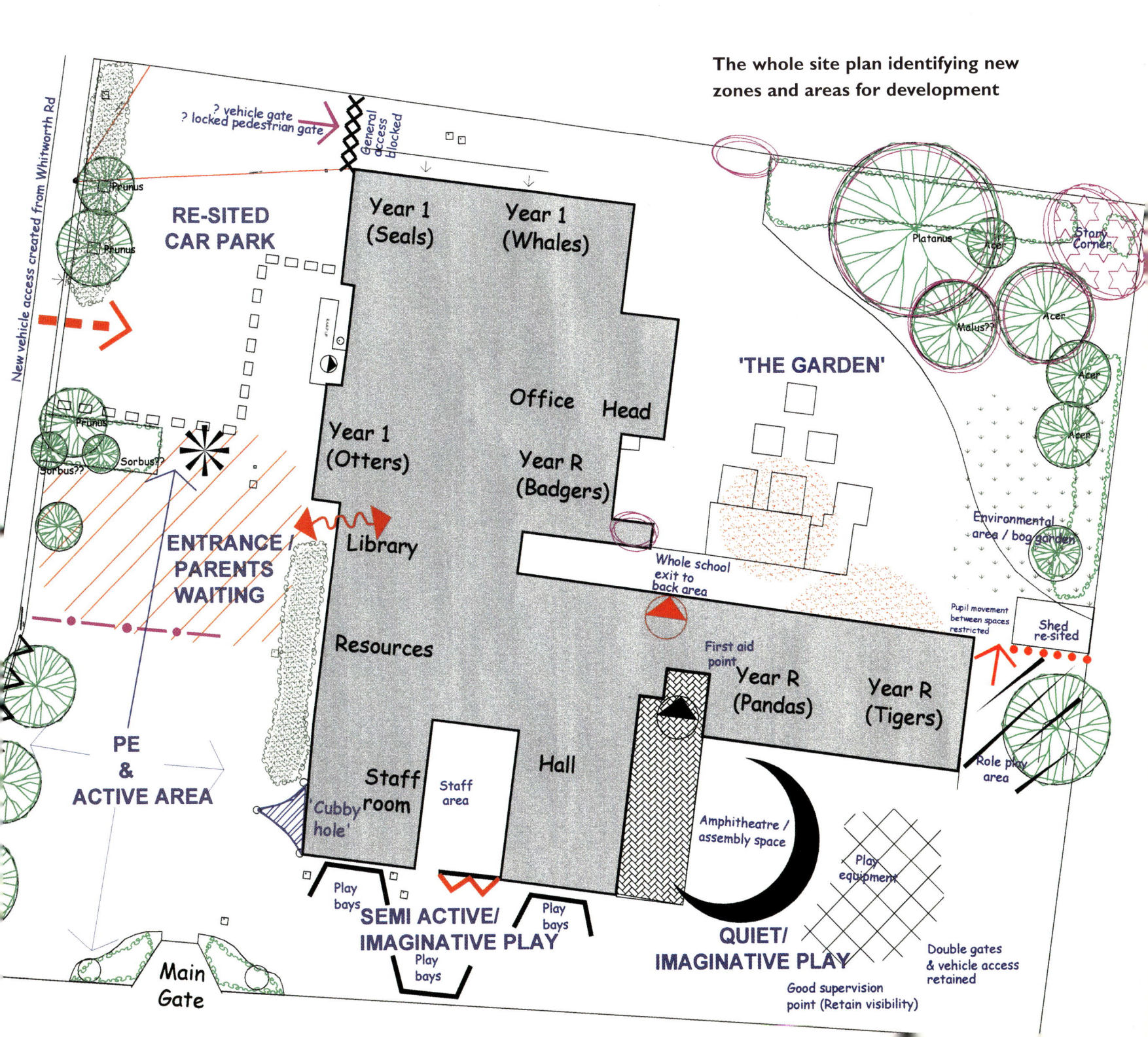

The whole site plan identifying new zones and areas for development

New vehicle access created from Whitworth Rd

? vehicle gate
? locked pedestrian gate
General access blocked

RE-SITED CAR PARK

Year 1 (Seals)
Year 1 (Whales)
Year 1 (Otters)
Office
Head
Year R (Badgers)

'THE GARDEN'

Platanus, Acer, Stony Corner, Malus??, Acer

ENTRANCE / PARENTS WAITING

Library

Whole school exit to back area

Environmental area / bog garden

Resources

Pupil movement between spaces restricted

Shed re-sited

First aid point
Year R (Pandas)
Year R (Tigers)

PE & ACTIVE AREA

Staff room
Staff area
Hall

'Cubby hole'

Role play area

Amphitheatre / assembly space

Play equipment

Play bays

SEMI ACTIVE/ IMAGINATIVE PLAY

Play bays

QUIET/ IMAGINATIVE PLAY

Main Gate

Good supervision point (Retain visibility)

Double gates & vehicle access retained

Active play area

How can we get there?

By the end of this stage the school wanted to have:

- detailed plans of the immediate changes
- a step-by-step action plan setting out targets and responsibilities.

Using a series of design/project briefs developed through the partnership, the landscape architect generated plans with the following zones:

Quiet imaginative play area – a sheltered space on the site of the existing car park, to provide a more appropriate place for quiet and imaginative play. The entrance would then be safe to use as a second main access to the school.

Semi-active and imaginative play – an area for specific playtime activities.

PE and active play – an area of open tarmac primarily for PE activities and active play.

Frontage – an attractive school frontage to Whitworth Road.

Entrance/parent waiting area – an attractive/welcoming entrance/waiting area.

Side area – a secure space that can be used as an outdoor area by the adjacent classrooms for sand and water play.

The garden – for early years provision, as an outdoor classroom and for imaginative/quiet play.

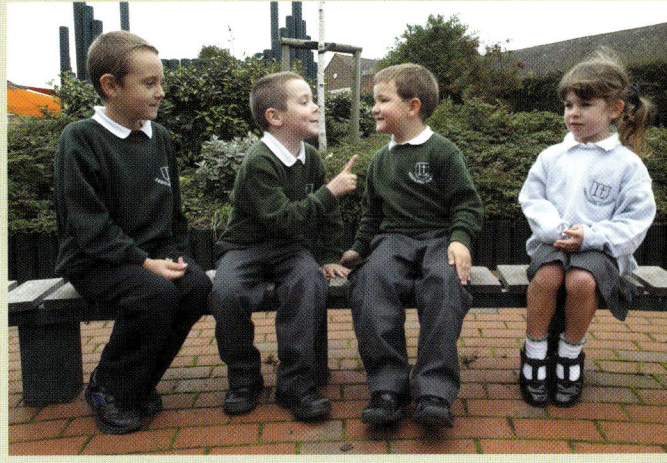

Making the changes

By the end of this stage the school wanted to have implemented the changes and be ready to think about future projects.

The work
The work was divided into four phases:

Phase 1 – The car park was relocated to the adjacent junior school. This enabled the former car park to be developed as quiet and semi-active play areas that included a stage, amphitheatre and raised imaginative play area.

Phases 2 and 3 – The development of the PE and active play area, along with the frontage and parents' waiting areas.

Phase 4 – The construction of the garden area.

Using and managing
Throughout this process the school established links with numerous partners to ensure they made best use of available expertise. The school tapped into a range of support that Hampshire brings together through its School Grounds Advisers Forum –
www.hants.gov.uk/environment
/schoolgroundsadvisers

During the final phase, the construction of 'the garden', the school had meetings with the Hampshire Gardens Trust to explore how they could develop ongoing support in the form of a 'Friends of' group.

The school views the development and use of its outdoor space as an on-going process, regularly reviewing its provision and searching for new ways to make best use of the grounds. The school has explored the potential of an arts project working with an artist within the garden. It also hopes to work with organisations such as the BTCV and the local Wildlife Trust to enrich the habitats within the nature area. Contacts such as these are available through the Hampshire School Grounds Advisers Forum.

The long-term commitment the school has made to develop its grounds has led it to look for opportunities to work in new and creative ways.

case study: Leesland Infant School 43

flowers

en Features

section **two**

This section looks first at some common design issues that affect all school grounds developments. That's followed by a look at some of the themes that schools and designers need to address and how school grounds can support each one, together with an explanation of the relating design issues.

designing and building

Common design issues

Central to designing and building school grounds is the need to instil ownership and respect among children and young people, the key community stakeholders for this space. Designers and teaching staff need to use their skills to ensure full participation, from the concept stage through creation to the ongoing maintenance and development beyond. This takes time, which should be factored into the design process. See the **developing school grounds** section for more information.

Individual school sites need individual solutions – schools and their communities are unique and should be the source for design inspiration. But there are some key design principles that need to be considered for any school:

- inspiration and variety
- choice and versatility
- access
- the natural environment
- management and maintenance
- security and safety.

In all cases, spatial relationships are crucial. Access, circulation and structural elements should be designed to bring spaces and features together.

▶ **Right**
Using colour and texture and incorporating pupils' artwork helps to reflect the ethos of the school and create a sense of place.

◀ **Below**
Standing stones and dry stone walling transform this much-used courtyard and reflect the local sense of place.

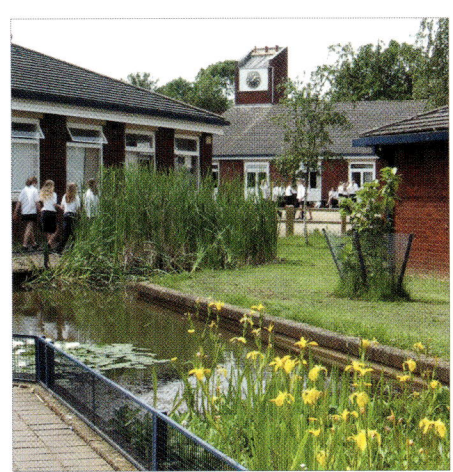

▶▶ **Far right**
Attractive landscaping can create a more positive and welcoming atmosphere.

Inspiration and variety

Schools are ultimately places for learning, and there's a need to understand the core ethos of learning to make school environments work. As well as the formal and informal curricula, all schools have a 'hidden curriculum' – all those messages given out by the feel of a place where children grow and develop. This is their environment, a reflection of how others view and value them, and an opportunity to provide many enhancing, health-giving experiences.

> "'Place making' is one of the best ways to promote positive behaviour and improve school grounds."
>
> Felicity Robinson,
> School Grounds Facilitator,
> Landscapes Naturally

Points to consider:

- A positive, welcoming and inspiring 'sense of place' should be created for everyone, which reflects and contributes to a school's identity.

- Users should feel nurtured and motivated to learn and teach – experiences outside the classroom can affect levels of concentration and well-being inside.

- School grounds should:
  - reflect the ethos and culture of the school through colour, texture, materials and shapes
  - reflect 'local distinctiveness'
  - use child-led ideas, graphics and colours
  - create comfortable, safe, welcoming, inspiring spaces
  - be integrated with the buildings on the site
  - be creative in the location and type of boundaries and space dividers.

- Schools choosing to specialise in one or more subjects may wish their school grounds to contribute to the specialism ethos.

section two: designing and building

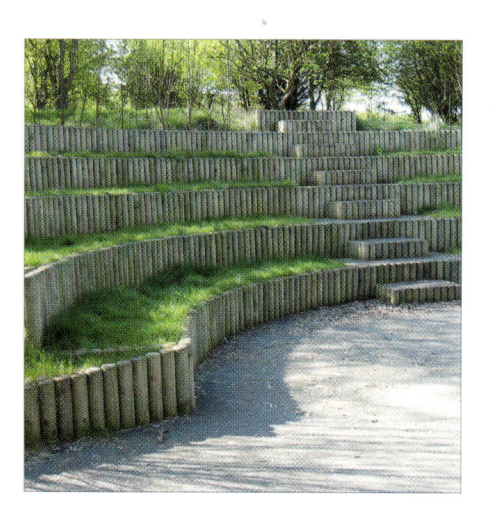

◀◀ Far left
This versatile space accommodates large audiences for performances but can be used for classes and smaller groups.

◀ Left
Equipment, planting, surfacing and low level fencing are used to define, divide and link spaces.

Choice and versatility

A school is a community of individuals and a place for social interaction, where large groups can be accommodated but where each pupil can find personal space if they need to.

Outdoor spaces need to support a variety of activities as well as the different needs of individual pupils.

Points to consider:

- Designers need to create a varied school grounds landscape that offers flexibility, with any feature having a number of potential uses, some of which can overlap:
  - quiet space for sitting and talking with friends
  - space away from others that can still be supervised
  - large open space for running and active play
  - enclosed secret space for hiding
  - spaces with potential for imagination and den building
  - gathering places and seating places
  - sheltered places
  - opportunities for community use.

- Place making and demands for a varied landscape mean that space needs to be well defined.

- Boundaries and space dividers don't need to be conventional – they could act as balancing beams, temporary screens, movable seating, playground markings, or flower tubs, for example.

- Textures and colours help to define spaces too.

Access

Access and circulation should be carefully considered in terms of efficiency, security and safety and the grounds zoned by their activity, clearly defining different uses.

Points to consider:

- Routes around the school will dictate flow of people and vehicles.

- Easy access to the outdoors makes it easier for teachers to use the outside more.

- The width and location of doorways and the size and surfacing of footpaths should reflect the volume of people using them at any time.

- All children – including those with special needs – should be able to access all parts of the site.

- There needs to be safe access for delivery and maintenance vehicles, dropping off points for buses and cars, and routes and facilities for pedestrians and cyclists.

- Careful location of delivery areas can mean no need for additional roads.

- Car parking is always an issue. Ideally, cars should be located off-site – but very often that's not possible. Car parking needs to be where it doesn't interfere with breaktime activities or movement around the school and is sited with health and safety in mind. Screening with a hedge or fence will prevent accidental damage to vehicles.

- The design should be linked to the School Traffic Plan.

designing school grounds

▶ **Right**
Designs should complement school travel plans and provide routes and facilities for cyclists and pedestrians.

▼ **Below**
Understanding and planning access and movement patterns of a site is fundamental to good design.

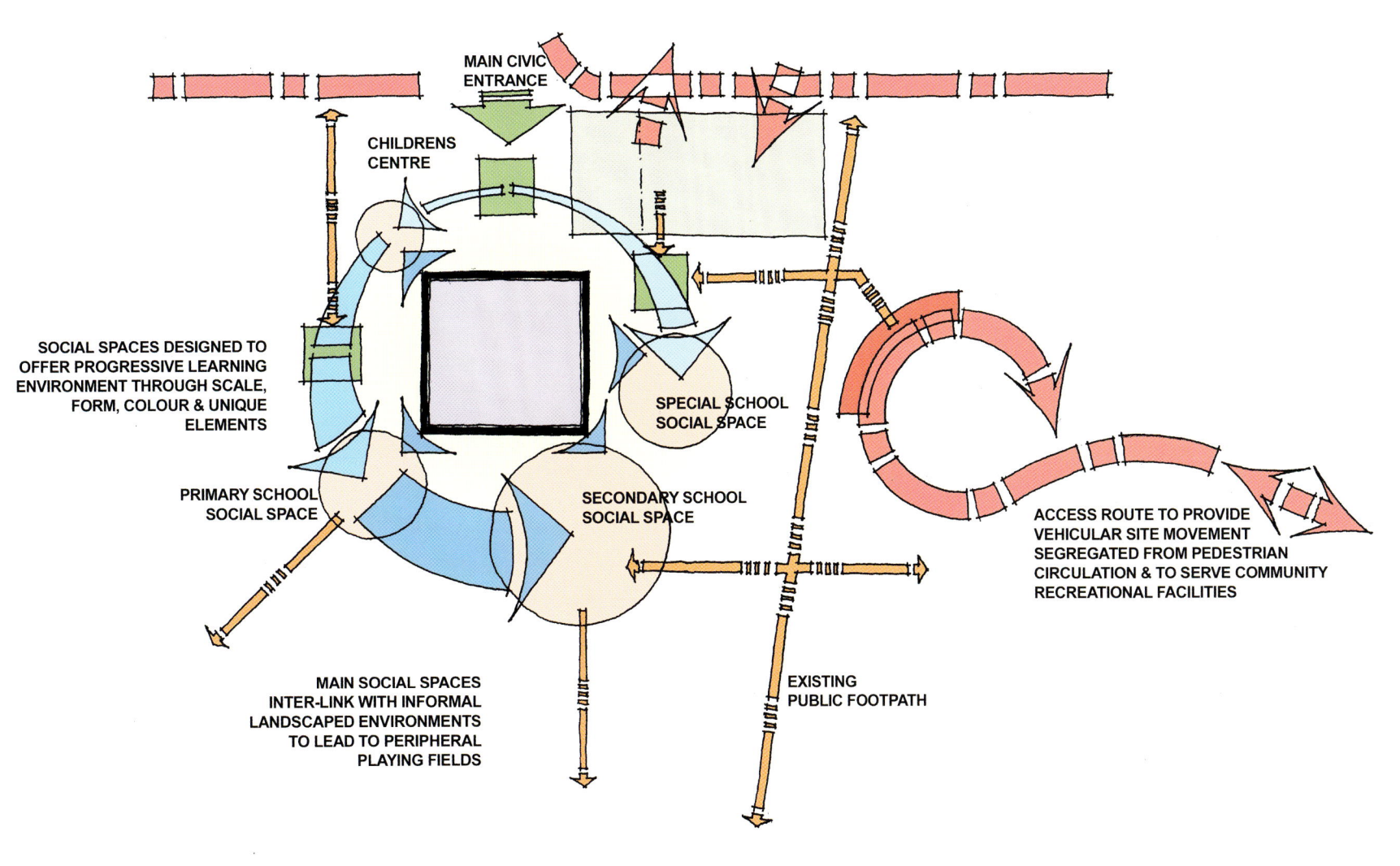

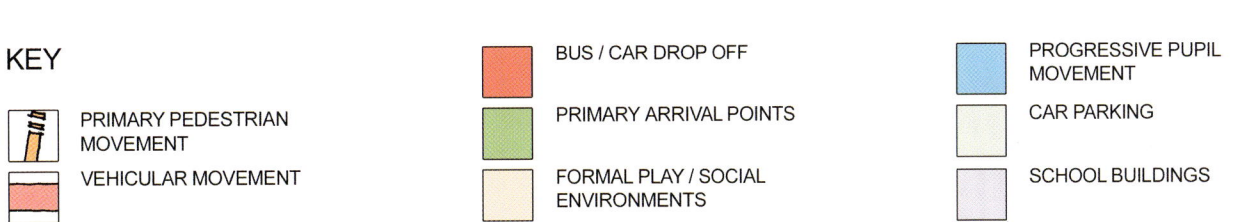

▶▶ **Far right**
Hard and soft landscaping create clear waymarking and provide a welcoming approach to this entrance.

MAIN CIVIC ENTRANCE

CHILDRENS CENTRE

SOCIAL SPACES DESIGNED TO OFFER PROGRESSIVE LEARNING ENVIRONMENT THROUGH SCALE, FORM, COLOUR & UNIQUE ELEMENTS

SPECIAL SCHOOL SOCIAL SPACE

PRIMARY SCHOOL SOCIAL SPACE

SECONDARY SCHOOL SOCIAL SPACE

ACCESS ROUTE TO PROVIDE VEHICULAR SITE MOVEMENT SEGREGATED FROM PEDESTRIAN CIRCULATION & TO SERVE COMMUNITY RECREATIONAL FACILITIES

MAIN SOCIAL SPACES INTER-LINK WITH INFORMAL LANDSCAPED ENVIRONMENTS TO LEAD TO PERIPHERAL PLAYING FIELDS

EXISTING PUBLIC FOOTPATH

KEY

PRIMARY PEDESTRIAN MOVEMENT

VEHICULAR MOVEMENT

BUS / CAR DROP OFF

PRIMARY ARRIVAL POINTS

FORMAL PLAY / SOCIAL ENVIRONMENTS

PROGRESSIVE PUPIL MOVEMENT

CAR PARKING

SCHOOL BUILDINGS

section two: designing and building

▶ **Left and below**
A combination of nature and man-made structures, temporary or permanent, provide shelter and shade.

The natural environment

Existing topography, vegetation, habitats and soil type, as well as related ecological processes, all influence the design and use of the school grounds. It's important to be sensitive to this and to work with it. For instance some mature trees may have preservation orders on them - any rebuilding of school grounds will need to bear this in mind.

There's more information in the section on **designing and building for sustainable outcomes**, and the DfES publications: *Sustainable schools – design primer* and *Design of sustainable schools – case studies*[9].

50 designing school grounds

▶ **Right**
Soft landscaping such as wooded boundaries and willow sculptures can be practical and aesthetic, providing habitat and enclosure.

◀ **Below**
Involvement of pupils in maintenance can help deliver the curriculum and encourage a sense of ownership.

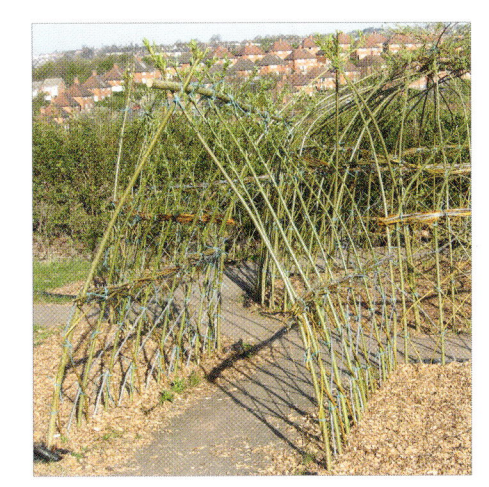

Points to consider:

- It's important to understand the micro-climates on the site, and how these affect use and behaviour.

- Additional shade and shelter – from sun, rain, wind and noise – can be provided in various ways: natural or man-made (or a combination of both), permanent or temporary. They may already exist from trees and buildings but the situation will change through the day and by the seasons.

- Soft landscaping is much valued and can be functional as well as aesthetic.

- Trees and other plants are invaluable – attractive, fun to plant and care for, enhancing curriculum opportunities.

- Bear in mind health and safety – consider choice, location and height of plants so there's no unnecessary risk to pupils and potential damage is limited.

section two: designing and building 51

◀ **Left**
Temporary structures can also provide great sensory experiences.

▼ **Below**
Lack of thought for the use and maintenance of this area soon resulted in a badly worn patch due to people cutting across.

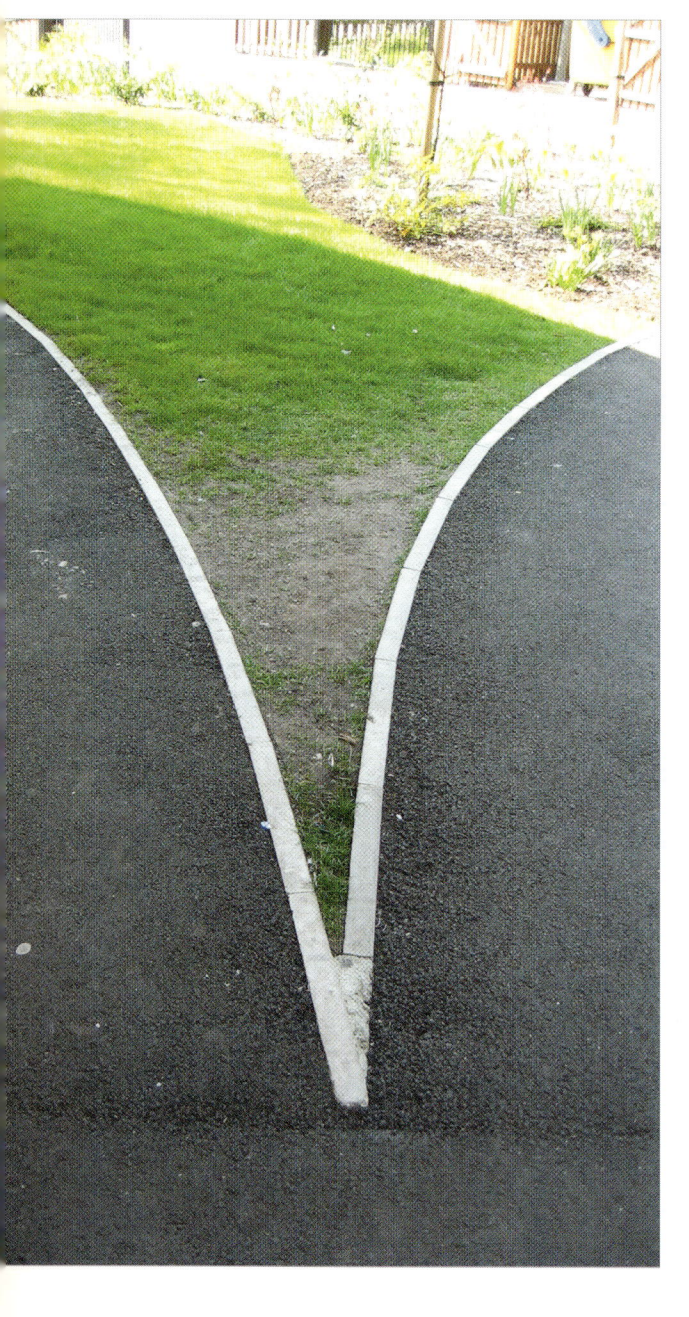

Management and maintenance

Considering and planning for the use, management and maintenance of the site as an integral part of the design is crucial to the long-term success and sustainability of the grounds. This includes ensuring that:

- teaching outside is written into schemes of work
- maintenance plans are properly written and updated
- provision for outdoor play is written into play and behaviour policies
- school grounds feature in development plans.

Points to consider:

- Schools may want to use maintenance of part of the grounds as a learning experience for pupils. This can be made easier by careful positioning of outdoor taps, for example, or creating raised beds for easy access for all.

- Longevity and robustness of outcomes, materials and equipment need to be taken into account. They won't only impact on the management and maintenance of the site, but will also have financial implications.

◢ **Right and below**
Security features such as fencing, window grilles and gates don't have to be 'prison-like', and can be a way of exhibiting pupils' creativity.

Security and safety

How the security of the school is handled is very important – high unsympathetic galvanised fences across the face of the school are liable to create a negative attitude in all who enter. Yet the security and safety of the site and its users is paramount. Guidance is available from local Police Architectural Liaison Officers and can be found in *Secured by Design*[10].

The safety of children within the grounds also needs to be balanced with the value of risk taking. See the **designing and building for healthy lifestyles** section for more information.

A place with plenty of lively activity, with the involvement of play facilitators and/or sports trainers, offers positive supervision through involvement rather than focusing on the more negative 'control' of behaviour.

Points to consider:

- A welcoming entrance that responds to the street with an above-basic fence will reflect the importance of the school in the community.
- Courtyards can provide surveillance black spots, which in turn make ideal break-in points – they are best when they can be secured so the school can leave their more valuable items such as artwork and furniture out at all times.
- Surveillance and supervision from staff in and out of school hours should be factored in – and how the space is managed.

There's further information in the **designing and building for positive behaviour** section.

section two: designing and building 53

Designing and building for...
learning and teaching

School grounds can provide an enormously valuable resource for learning and teaching – for any subject, at short notice and for little or no cost. So it's vitally important that their capacity to support curriculum delivery and opportunities for learning through play are considered in their design.

The new *Manifesto for Education Outside the Classroom*[11] will bring together many different interests to promote its value, including school grounds.

To help staff get the most out of their grounds for teaching and play, designers need to talk with them about their needs, how they use the grounds now and how they might use them in the future. Exploring the national curriculum[12] and QCA[13] or school Schemes of Work will help designers and teachers see the scope of possibilities for lessons outside.

Children learn in different ways. Some learn best through seeing or hearing but many, particularly boys and some pupils with special needs, learn best through doing.

Outdoors, children continue to learn through listening and looking but there are also many potential opportunities to take part in hands-on learning. The outdoors can have several advantages for practical learning – there's more space; noise and mess are often seen as less serious issues; and children can try out real activities. It's often when some of these learning styles are combined during first-hand experiences that the best learning takes place, because all the senses are being used.

The school grounds can benefit learning and teaching in three key ways, by providing:

- an alternative to an internal teaching space
- specialist facilities that it is difficult/impossible to provide inside a building
- an environment for experiential learning.

An alternative teaching space

Creating practical outdoor teaching spaces

Some schools develop spaces where a whole class can join together. Many teachers value this type of space so that they can gather their pupils in one place for whole-class presentation or discussion. It also provides a focus for pupils and somewhere equipment can be left for them to collect. Spaces for smaller groups can be equally valuable.

Points to consider:

- Factor in the practicalities of taking classes outside, with spaces for different sizes of groups, creating places for sitting and writing, or providing storage spaces so that equipment is easily accessible.
- Include sensible risk management, so that learning and teaching can take place outside the classroom.

▶ **Right**
This seating is specifically designed for young children.

▶▶ **Far right**
This amphitheatre accommodates large audiences for performances or whole classes for lessons.

◀ **Below**
This seat and surrounding area are for a story-teller and audience.

- Spaces need to be:
  - near enough to the school to use easily but far enough away not to disturb other classes
  - next to a feature that is frequently studied (eg a pond)
  - providing shade and shelter at different times of year
  - fulfilling a particular use (eg story-telling)
  - appropriate for the age of pupils they need to accommodate
  - clearly defined
  - for a whole class or smaller numbers.

- The topography of the site can be used to good effect and even determine the design of seating – for example, an amphitheatre-style area in a sloping site.

- If the seats have no shelter, the school could make their own cushions to use even when the seats are damp.

- Trees can be a focal point for seating as they provide natural shade – they can also be a good basis for tree houses.

section two: designing and building for… learning and teaching   55

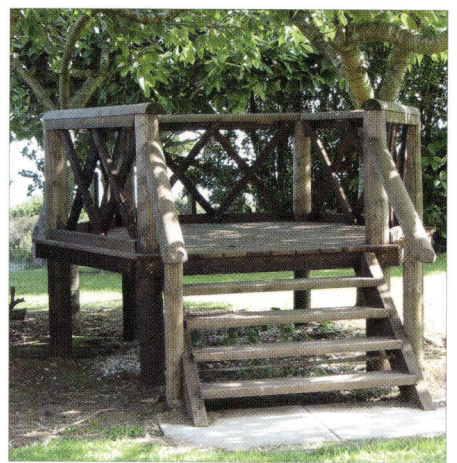

◀◀ **Far left**
Ponds are good for learning about science – and inspiring.

◀ **Left**
A crow's nest seating area – a starting point for story-telling and literacy work.

◢ **Below**
This yellow planting bed sparks inspiration.

Using the grounds to inspire

While the grounds can be a wonderful location to teach in, they can also become an inspiration for different lessons. Even the most barren grounds demonstrate seasonal change – but grounds with a variety of elements such as a range of colours, textures, foliage, habitats, spaces, micro-climates and topography can be used as a basis for many more starting points for lessons.

Points to consider:

- Given the sense of open space invariably conveyed by sports pitches, emphasis elsewhere can be on varying degrees of enclosure.

- An amphitheatre, glade, dell or outdoor room can provide complete visual barriers, filtered glimpses and open views – these offer great potential for separation between active pursuits (such as ball games or chasing), passive group activities (such as chatting), and passive activities for individuals (such as reading or reflecting).

- The ways these spaces are linked is equally important in extending the range of educational opportunities.

▶ **Right**
Children developing their creative skills.

▼ **Below**
Seeing birds and wildlife is more memorable than studying them in a book.

section two: designing and building for… learning and teaching 57

◀◀ **Far left**
Covered space outside these classrooms allows year-long use.

◀ **Left**
Specialised play equipment accommodates wheelchair access; standard equipment may also be suitable for special needs.

▼ **Below**
Particular attention was given at this primary school to how classes could access the outdoors.

58　designing school grounds

▲ **Right and below**
Existing buildings can make good equipment stores and (right) smaller containers strategically placed provide easy access.

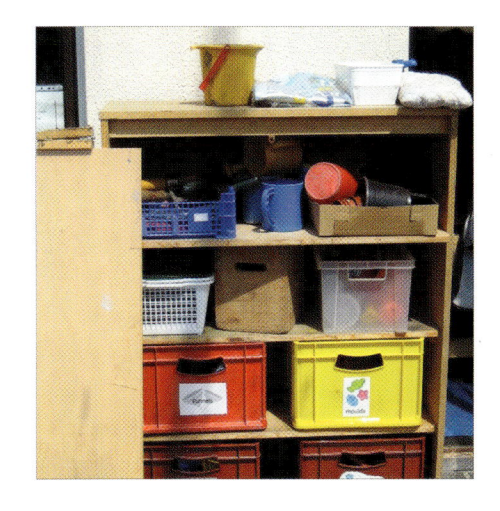

Access

Easy access to the outdoors from the classroom enables teachers to use the outside as often as possible. For the early years sector, free flow between inside and out is essential. But even for older pupils, direct access to the outside from their classrooms means that more frequent use of the outdoors is more likely.

Points to consider:

- All children in the school need to be able to access the resources in the grounds. This doesn't mean there shouldn't be an element of challenge in getting to or using places or features. There's information about access for pupils with special needs in the **designing and building for different sectors and needs** part of this section.

- There's a wide range of play equipment for children with physical disabilities, including swings and roundabouts for those using wheelchairs and tactile elements for those with visual impairment. But don't overlook more standard equipment — or the creation of bespoke elements designed to meet the specific needs of pupils.

- Equipment should be stored where it's easily accessible, possibly next to where it's most often used, and it must be secure — especially where other people use the site (whether officially or unofficially).

section two: designing and building for... learning and teaching   59

▼ **Below**
This secondary school maths maze was designed to be used in lessons as well as at break times.

Specialist facilities

Physical education
Much of the PE and school sports (PESS) curriculum is taught outside, and the space it needs should be factored in when the outdoors is being developed. Along with games and athletics, Outdoor and Adventurous Activities is the topic most likely to be taken outside.

Points to consider:

- PESS facilities provided at school-only level can be enhanced to provide local club-level provision – which can potentially provide third party revenue to cover their additional cost and at the same time integrate the school more closely into the community.

- Developments should be made in conjunction with the local authority sports strategy and can be supported by school sports coordinators.

- These coordinators also play an important role in developing out-of-hours opportunities, and in linking schools to local clubs.

▶ **Right**
A polytunnel used where horticulture skills are taught.

▼ **Below**
Wind chimes and other outdoor musical instruments add a new dimension to lessons.

- There are likely to be many areas of the grounds that can also be used for other activities without restricting use for PESS – these should be taken into account at the briefing stage.

Other curriculum-related features

Some schools may need curriculum-specific features such as:

- horticulture: polytunnels, raised beds, growing areas
- agriculture: areas for livestock and hard landscaped construction features
- arts and music: musical instruments, a performance area
- maths and science: a maths maze, a wind turbine, a dipping platform[14].

section two: designing and building for… learning and teaching

◀ **Left**
This willow maze provides active, quiet or imaginative play experiences.

▼ **Below**
Well-designed spaces, with permanent or temporary equipment, provide endless play opportunities.

Experiential learning

Learning through play

Play is an important part of pupils' learning and development experience at school. It's the way young children learn in particular, but it's crucial for all age groups. Through play, children learn about themselves, others and the world around them. They learn through experimenting, taking risks, undertaking challenges and finding out where their limits lie. And they need to be given opportunities to stretch themselves within a safe environment – such as the school grounds. An enriched play environment can be achieved by providing a variety of opportunities.[15]

Points to consider:

- Play equipment needs to be suitable for the age using it, robust enough to withstand constant use (and possibly some unauthorised use) and it shouldn't restrict children's imaginations.

- Play equipment that's versatile and can be adapted by the user is the most useful.

- Small mobile pieces of play equipment will need to be stored when they're not in use.

- In all schools there will be concerns about pupils' safety. These do need to be taken into account but shouldn't prevent pupils' adventurous and creative play. A thorough risk assessment needs to be carried out to ensure that play is challenging without being unnecessarily dangerous.

- Playground markings and murals can also support play. While standard elements can be bought, pupils may also design their own, trialling them in chalk first.

- Friendship stops or buddy benches and/or playground squads can help manage playtimes in primary schools. Friendship stops can be designed specifically for an individual school and their location and design should be decided in discussion with pupils and staff.

designing school grounds

Real project scenario

The real-life design process can develop skills in devising solutions, thinking creatively, solving problems and working as a team. All these are key in developing sustainable practice. See the section on **developing school grounds** for more information.

AT A GLANCE

PRACTICAL OUTDOOR TEACHING SPACE

- Create well-defined, appropriately-sized outdoor classrooms
- Consider places for whole classes (approx 30) and smaller groups
- Consider access, location from classroom, logistics of using the space
- Consider storage and pick-up places for equipment needed
- Make use of existing features like trees and slopes
- Design in seating, shelter and shade
- Design in focus and features

PLAY

- Create versatile, adaptable spaces
- Consider criteria for an enriched play environment
- Build integrated indoor/outdoor spaces
- Allow for experimentation, imagination and challenge
- Balance safety and challenge
- Consider special educational needs

SPECIFIC CURRICULUM-RELATED FEATURES INCLUDE:

- Polytunnel
- Raised beds
- Livestock pens
- Maths maze or trail
- Woodland trail
- Musical instruments
- Wind turbine
- Pond dipping platform
- Performance area
- Story-telling circle
- Hoops
- Nets
- Wall targets
- Floor markings

Designing and building for...
healthy lifestyles

Physical activity and active play

Well-designed and -managed school grounds can benefit children and young people in four key ways, by:

- providing opportunities for physical activity and active play
- contributing to emotional well-being
- providing opportunities to grow and learn about food
- integrating safety, risk and challenge into school grounds.

It's important to consider how time spent in the grounds will be managed – and how this will work with the design of the site. Children could be involved in rule-making, potentially through curriculum work, and have a role in designing site notices.

From a health perspective[16], children and young people should take part in one hour of at least moderate intensity physical activity every day. In addition schools need to provide at least two hours of high quality PE and school sport each week for all their pupils. They should also consider the contribution that they need to make to the long-term ambition of four hours of sport per week for all pupils[17]. Physical activity improves concentration, enhances academic performance, develops skills and attitudes, improves self-esteem and promotes lifelong participation in physical activity. Schools have an important role to play in helping to increase levels of physical activity through the formal and informal curriculum – and the grounds provide a safe opportunity to take part.

Daily routine and school ethos

- Physical activity should be seen in its widest sense and integrated into the daily life of the school.
- Grounds designed to allow easy access and a stimulating environment will encourage lessons to be taken outside, increasing pupils' activity.
- There needs to be a range of physical activity opportunities for all ages, levels and genders, and all should have equal opportunity to take part. This doesn't mean that the whole space should be active at all times.
- Well-thought-out and well-placed space definers, which themselves may be useful pieces of equipment, ensure that robust games don't take over the whole area.

◀ **Right and below**
Playground markings prompt active and imaginative play, and problem solving.

School grounds features and equipment

- School grounds designs should incorporate features to promote active play, such as traversing walls, playground markings and fixed play equipment.
- Storage for temporary equipment is also important.
- Features such as ball walls and markings can be used during curriculum and non-curriculum time.
- Energising colours and patterns can enhance and define areas of 'activity'.
- New equipment must meet the relevant British and European standards for equipment design and the need for impact-absorbing, or safety surfaces.[18,19]
- Equipment should be located in more than one area if possible to avoid a 'honeypot' effect.
- Play equipment needs to be suitable for the age using it, robust and versatile. See **designing and building for learning and teaching** for further information on play.
- Site features and materials not designed specifically for play can still provide opportunities for exercise, play and aesthetic improvements, though they come with their own risks and challenges. For example, loose logs, railway sleepers, tyres and rocks can provide informal seating areas and valuable balancing activities, especially suitable for children with some specific learning difficulties. These all need to be cleaned thoroughly and potential hazards removed.

section two: designing and building for... healthy lifestyles 65

◀ **Left**
Fixed play equipment encourages individual and collaborative physical play.

▼ **Below**
Where space is limited, 'traversing walls' develop upper body strength and add colour and interest to a plain wall.

66 designing school grounds

Right and below
In a range of spaces pupils have choices and opportunities to interact and behave in a variety of ways.

Emotional well-being

Many factors contribute to the emotional well-being of children and young people. But the impact of the local environment shouldn't be underestimated.

Providing choice

An outdoor space should provide a range of opportunities for different types of behaviour.

The use of colour, textures, details and soft planting, particularly sensory plants, can create calm atmospheres. This provides children with the opportunity to choose quiet reflection and to relax – and can be a favourite with teachers working with small groups.

Points to consider:

- Grounds need to be designed so that pupils develop a positive relationship with certain spaces at certain times and develop a sense of 'place'. For example, a place:

    - to sit quietly on your own or with friends, to read, chat or simply watch the world go by

    - to play and use your imagination

    - to run around and play games and sport

    - to hide and make a den

    - to perform

    - to enjoy your break-time snack

    - that's dry, shaded and sheltered

    - that is safe.

◀◀ **Far left**
Storage is vital but sheds needn't be boring.

◀ **Left**
Raised beds make good use of the perimeter area.

▶ **Below**
Pupils can be involved at all stages of garden design.

Growing food

Through growing and nurturing plants and animals, children also learn practical and social skills and improve their physical well-being. They begin to understand where their food comes from and the interdependence of people, plants and animals.

Growing food in the school grounds is also a valuable way of supporting the concept of healthy eating. Growing food links to a range of curriculum areas and can lead to the achievement of vocational qualifications.

Points to consider:

- Plants can be grown irrespective of space – in plots, raised beds and containers.
- Many schools also have greenhouses and polytunnels.
- Whatever the space available, when you're deciding where to grow food, you need to take into account:
    - **micro-climate** – ideally a sunny area that's reasonably sheltered from strong winds
    - **water** – ensure good access to water and adequate drainage

68 designing school grounds

Far left
Herbs grown in cut-off plastic bottles on a pergola make good use of limited space.

Left
Creative containers add interest to planting space.

- **contents** – consider a specific plot for food crops or mix with a shrub or flower border

- **orientation** – plots should run north to south, allowing maximum sunlight on all plants through the day, planting in rows east to west

- **access** – consider width and surfacing for paths surrounding plots and raised beds in particular to ensure access for all pupils and necessary equipment

- **maintenance** – consider how the space will be managed and maintained during school holidays, for example whether direct access will be required.

- When you're choosing plants, you need to think about:

  - growing and harvesting time, and how these link with term and holiday dates

  - use of drought-tolerant plants

  - amount of maintenance required

  - how the products could be used

  - sensory aspects, such as colour, texture, scent.

GROWING SCHOOLS PROGRAMME[20]

This programme aims to support and encourage schools to use the 'outdoor classroom' as a resource for all curriculum subjects, for pupils of all ages and abilities. Using school grounds for learning and growing is an important strand of Growing Schools. The programme also promotes field studies and visits to farms, country estates, botanical gardens and national parks.

The most obvious subjects include Science KS1 to 4 – 'Life processes and living things'; Geography KS1 to 3 – 'Knowledge and understanding of environmental change and sustainable development'; Citizenship KS3 – 'Environmental Projects'. But all subjects can be enriched by using the outdoors to give pupils experiential learning opportunities.

Many schools that have developed gardens or keep animals at school use them as a resource to teach other curriculum subjects such as Maths (weighing a sheep, or calculating the milk intake of lambs), Design and Technology (making carts to transport pumpkins from the pumpkin patch to the classroom or cooking pancakes made with eggs laid by the school hens). The DfES' Five Year Strategy for Children and Learners encourages teachers to make learning more flexible and imaginative, and make better use of out-of-classroom opportunities. It also suggests that schools should become environmentally sustainable, with a school garden or other means for children to explore the natural world.

▶ **Right**
Learning about the Great Fire of London in a practical way also taught these primary school children about fire safety.

▶▶ **Far right**
Textured surfacing can add interest but remember safety!

Safety, risk and challenge

Designing out danger

Health and safety (H&S) in school grounds is a major consideration for all sites. Appropriate risk and challenge are necessary and should be managed in a way that minimises danger. Learning to manage risk is a vital aspect of a child's development – and a degree of challenge allows them to recognise and take acceptable risks. But you will need to identify potentially dangerous situations so that unnecessary risk can be designed out. Two examples are described below.

Textured surfacing

Textured surfaces can add visual interest and texture – but can also be a trip hazard.

- Think about how the surface will be used, how often and by whom.
- Textured surfacing should be used to highlight areas but not used in areas of high traffic.
- Textured surfacing can also be used to reduce risk. For example, it can be used to create rumble strips on pathways where young children use wheeled toys. These can act as environmental 'alerts' to the children to take care and watch out for pedestrians.

Ponds

Ponds are very useful for teaching science and water safety and are popular features in grounds. Raised ponds work well as part of a larger habitat area with year-round access.

Good design, along with effective management and maintenance, is essential to prevent unnecessary risks.

- Design and locate the pond to be obvious.
- Make sure edges are sloping and well defined.
- Provide a suitable area, such as a deck, for dipping.
- Locate the pond where children cannot reach it without supervision, such as in a courtyard or fenced area. Fencing should be robust and secure.
- Cover the pond with steel mesh if children have access without supervision.

Designing in challenge and risk taking

Well-designed and challenging school grounds, graduated to cater for appropriate levels of ability, can offer a safer environment than a boring, flat, unstimulating site. In a challenging environment, children will be able to test their abilities, learn from their mistakes and stretch themselves further to develop their physical and mental skills.

Points to consider:

- Risk management should be discussed at an early stage of the project.
- Each school has a member of staff responsible for health and safety as part of their health and safety (H&S) policy, which should include both outdoor and indoor environments.
- In most cases the ultimate responsibility lies with the local authority, which publishes its own H&S policy that local schools need to follow.
- There's no standard policy for H&S for all schools in the UK, although schools as workplaces are subject to the Health and Safety at Work Act 1974[21].

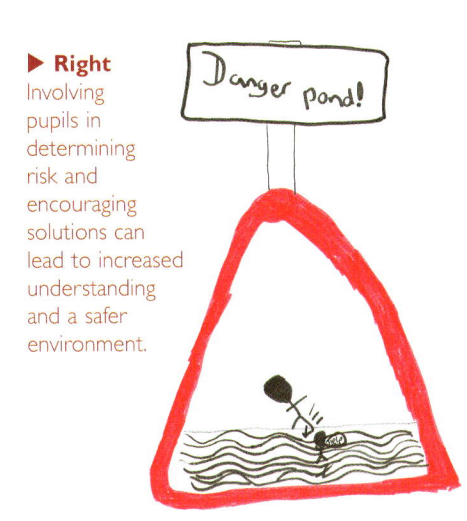

▶ **Right**
Involving pupils in determining risk and encouraging solutions can lead to increased understanding and a safer environment.

You can get further advice and information from the Health and Safety Executive and organisations such as the Royal Society for the Prevention of Accidents (RoSPA) and the National Playing Fields Association (NPFA).

Site assessments

Site assessments at the start and throughout the design and build of the development are essential to identify current and potential risks. Existing sites can provide vital information that can be used to develop either the same site or new ones. Staff and pupil knowledge, accident records and community opinions should all inform the design process.

AT A GLANCE

PRINCIPLES

PHYSICAL ACTIVITY AND ACTIVE PLAY

- Provide a variety of active play opportunity – grading physical challenge, making attractive to different users
- Avoid 'honeypot' locations
- Zone and define the space for active play

EMOTIONAL WELL-BEING

- Respect the need for personal space, and cater for the different spaces and opportunities children need for social interaction
- Create stillness and calm – make use of colour, texture, planting

GROWING FOOD

- Use the right locations and orientation for good growing

HEALTH AND SAFETY

- Create a challenging but safe environment

RISK AND CHALLENGE

- Build in shade and shelter
- Make use of safety surfacing

MORE IDEAS

ACTIVE FEATURES

- Traversing walls
- Playground markings
- Fixed play equipment
- Temporary play equipment
- Ball walls
- Balancing beams
- Fitness trails
- Logs – stepping stones

'WELL' FEATURES

- Shelters
- Sensory gardens and peace gardens
- Quiet seating areas
- Water features

GROWING FEATURES

- Vegetable plots, raised beds pots and containers
- Greenhouse
- Polytunnel
- Herb garden
- Kitchen garden
- Orchard
- Chicken coop

Designing and building for...
positive behaviour

'Place making' is one of the best ways to promote positive behaviour and improve school grounds. It involves creating places that promote a sense of ownership, respect and responsibility – places where activity is appropriate to the location, reducing the risk of aggression, boredom, conflict and damage.

Behaviour is influenced by a range of interlinked design and management decisions. Each site has its own unique solutions but a common important factor is the initial involvement of students in a community safety and behaviour audit. Professionals skilled in site analysis – and working closely with young people to ensure full participation – can help to reduce costs associated with site damage by identifying and preventing potential risks. Indeed, Crime Prevention Through Environmental Design (CPTED) principles applied to school sites have shown how important it is to involve young people in site risk assessment.[22]

Research[23] shows that the design of school grounds can subtly influence the attitudes and behaviour of children and young people, with benefits in four key areas:

- reducing opportunities for conflict
- developing environments conducive to social interaction
- reducing damage, and opportunities for theft
- facilitating surveillance/supervision and capable guardians.

Reducing opportunities for conflict

Movement generators, routes, nodes and congestion points all need to be identified for a clear idea of flows of people during the daily pattern of school activity. Conflict often arises at these points and young people feel intimidated.

"...crowded... people push... lots of people try to get by... get pushed and hurt... dark... narrow and squashy... congestion... dirty... fights and crowding... can't see through... yuk... loud..."

Year 7 and 11 pupils

▶ **Right**
Seating at entrances or along narrow routes can provoke conflict between those gathering and those passing through.

▶▶ **Far right**
New paving, lighting and bright walls have improved this former trouble spot.

◂ **Below**
Traffic calming – a cobble 'rumble strip' along a nursery path.

Points to consider:

- Places should be designed with well-defined routes, spaces and entrances that provide for convenient movement, with areas where pupils can gather without intimidating others.

- Young people have a habit of gathering around doorways – and to an extent this needs to be catered for, so as not to impede access and provoke aggression.

- Avoid seating perches and litter traps along routes and provide seating where it's appropriate.

- Paths need to be wide enough to allow for the fact that children and young people tend to move around in wide groups.

- Paved corners (rather than right angles with trip rails) can reduce jostling at junctions and minimise the damage caused by corner cutting.

- It's best to reduce congestion around PE equipment or playprop stores – open up these entrances and use wide double doors.

- Ensure that there are at least two exits to any enclosure – in shelters, gazebos, fenced climbing frames for instance – or a very wide entrance, to avoid anyone being trapped or intimidated.

section two: designing and building for… positive behaviour

▼ **Below**
Territoriality can be positive with sufficient places for pupils to gather.

▼ **Bottom**
Letting students manipulate loose structures such as benches promotes positive behaviour.

Developing environments conducive to social interaction

Structure and zoning

The definition and structure of a place is important. Appropriate activities within these places need to be clear, whether they are ball games, climbing, sitting or exploring. Sites that are more 'legible', with well-defined routes, a 'sense of place' and a clear purpose, and where adjacent uses don't clash, reduce the risk of conflicts between users.

The adoption of spaces by year groups can be a cause of conflict but are inevitable and often necessary. The needs of different groups can be met by providing sufficient, well-designed gathering spaces for all groups. If there are not enough spaces, older or dominant children will adopt them, inducing tensions and hierarchies.

The type of places often identified as worrying for young people are places where there's little definition of place or activity – *"…bleak… desolate… boring… no teachers… fights… bullies"* Year 7 and 11 pupils – with purposeless roaming around the site more apparent at breaktimes.

A variety of types of place can help to promote social interaction – places for large groups, more intimate places where small groups can chat, places where individuals can *"be miserable if they want to"* or places to *"have a headache in peace"*. Primary child.

Micro-climate

- The influence of micro-climate on behaviour can sometimes be underestimated. It's easier to relax in sheltered, warmer places in cold weather and shady places in warm weather.

- Wide open expanses and windswept spaces encourage chasing games; other types of space should also be on offer.

- Consider the orientation of shelters, the degree of enclosure of places, protection from the prevailing wind and eddying currents around buildings.

▶ **Right**
This seating has different levels to accommodate students' need to be up high and in informal groups.

▶▶ **Far right**
Well-designed social seating is important at any age, promoting positive behaviour.

Design 'grain', colour and mood

- Colour, texture and pattern can be used to define areas and promote particular types of activity.
- Calming colours, relaxed patterns, sensory details and finger mazes help to promote reflective activity, and fine-grain detail is appropriate in these spaces, where it can be appreciated. Conversely, energising colours can distinguish the more active areas.

Points to consider:

- Zoning can make a significant contribution in otherwise bleak, expansive, multi-purpose playground spaces and can help define the structure.
- Zone boundaries need not be fences. They can be surface paving changes, texture, colour, signage, planting, temporary or modular barriers.
- Good design is crucial to ensuring that access, circulation and structural elements of the landscape work to bring all the spaces together.
- Zoning by activity rather than by age can be very useful, especially in primary schools, with a continuum of active to passive being the ideal in most circumstances.
- Zoning is a good way to ensure that quiet areas are undisturbed. Sensory noise such as water can be calming and can also act as 'white noise' to mask unwanted sound. Vision is a factor — if you can't see the noise generator, such as the street, its perceived impact is reduced.
- Places with good views of other activities allow children to be part of something without taking part. Many feel more comfortable being 'up high' and with their backs protected, for solitary or group viewing of activities. Children often like to sit on the back of benches for this reason, so design to allow for this preference.
- Children and young people often like to be able to have a degree of control over their spaces. Rearranging the furniture can sometimes be enough to help define a sense of place, or create a vantage point/spectator position.
- Experimental layouts can be very helpful to assess configurations that best encourage positive behaviours. These can be monitored through observation, time-lapse filming, vox pops, and focus groups and the results incorporated in new permanent designs.

'**Zoneparcs**' is a programme which aims to transform traditionally uninspiring primary school playgrounds into vibrant, exciting and welcoming spaces for children. Playgrounds are zoned into three distinct areas using:

- the Red Zone for traditional, active sports
- the Blue Zone, a multi-activity area for children to play alone, in pairs, in groups or in teams
- the Yellow Zone, a quiet area where children can read or play board games.

Combined with careful management, the playgrounds have resulted in increased activity and enjoyment among children. Further details about the joint Youth Sport Trust/Nike/DfES programme are set out in a DfES booklet *Primary Playground Development*. Copies of the document can be obtained from DfES publications at dfes@prolog.uk.com quoting reference PE/ZP.

▶ **Right**
A survey by primary pupils of current activities and safety issues.

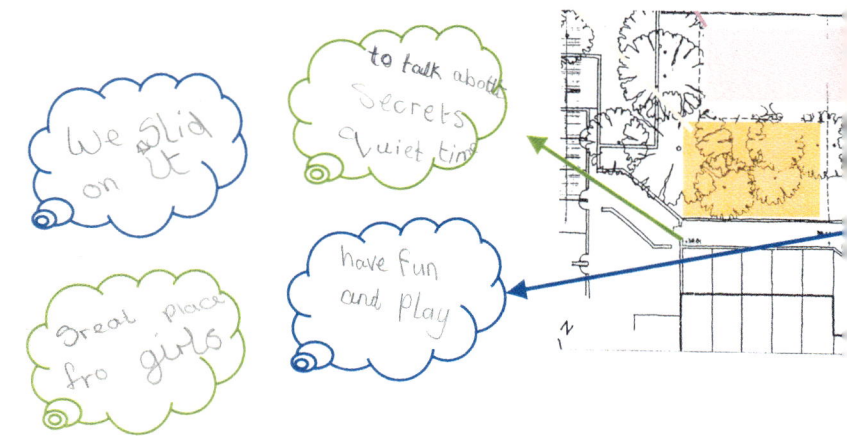

Reducing damage and opportunities for theft

Ownership, respect

Involvement in design and ongoing decisions, modelling the use of spaces in the curriculum, and regular opportunities to make your mark, or as one Year 6 pupil put it, *"leaving a present for the next group of children,"* are all features of developments with less subsequent damage.

Points to consider:

- Young people need to be involved in the design phases and the ongoing management and maintenance, through work-related learning and/or club-based activities. See the **design** section for more details.

- Casual damage can be caused by normal behaviour if the facilities aren't sufficiently robust and designed with their use in mind.

- Wilful damage can be reduced if there's greater variety in the activities on offer to reduce boredom.

- Very quick repairs and graffiti removal demonstrate zero tolerance and prevent a decline towards further damage.

Secure storage

Storage units can be crime generators but are essential in grounds, especially child-accessible stores for PESS equipment and play props.

Points to consider:

- Storage units can have slatted open fronts so that intruders can see there's nothing to interest them and that they are not worth breaking into.

- Where secure storage is required the Crime Prevention Design Adviser or Architectural Liaison Officer can advise on units with a Secured by Design rating.

The **glossary** has further information.

Surveillance, supervision and 'capable guardians'

Supervision (which is overt) and surveillance (which is more subtle and less obvious) should each be considered in the design of an outdoor space. Both can have a significant influence on the success of a site and both can be considered 'capable guardians' by children and young people.

Points to consider:

- Photo surveys by young people have highlighted locations where the students identified a lack of surveillance or 'eyes on the scene'. These include hidden corners and 'inactive edges', which can often be addressed through integrated design of the indoor and outdoor spaces.

- Many areas can be classic 'inactive edges' — for example, the blank walls of large buildings such as sports halls, even though there are windows. This is sometimes because the windows are relatively high, above bench height, and don't afford a good view of the outside. Where possible, the building design should avoid large, blank walls next to activity areas.

"…dead-end-dangerous… hiding places… out of bounds… no teachers around… not monitored… people in classrooms, but no-one would hear you… lots of messing around… people try to stop you… wasps!…"

Year 7 pupils

- The site layout should maximise opportunities for natural surveillance, making positive use of overlooking, interaction and encounters with staff and other students.
- Staff rooms and offices should be positioned if possible where they can have a surveillance function.
- Spaces and buildings beyond the school site, such as adjacent roads, footpaths, properties and other buildings, may also influence surveillance.
- Recessed doorways need visibility splays – and mirrors can help to provide visual access to difficult places.
- Children put faith in CCTV but are sometimes unaware that it's usually only passively monitored.

AT A GLANCE

REDUCING OPPORTUNITIES FOR CONFLICT
- Consider movement patterns
- Reduce congestion points
- Provide appropriate seating locations
- Use wide paved paths
- Avoid right-angled corners
- Open up entrances and use wide double doors

DEVELOPING ENVIRONMENTS CONDUCIVE TO SOCIAL INTERACTION
- Create a sense of place
- Provide a variety of spaces – for different group sizes, ages and activities
- Clearly define spaces
- Use alternatives to fixed barriers
- Use colours, textures and patterns to suit the activity
- Provide vantage points
- Use experimental layouts
- Design for the micro-climate

REDUCING DAMAGE AND OPPORTUNITIES FOR THEFT
- Ensure full participation to encourage ownership and respect
- Provide for a variety of activities to reduce boredom
- Design for robustness
- Repair quickly to minimise vandalism
- Provide secure storage

SURVEILLANCE/SUPERVISION
- Maximise opportunities for natural surveillance from within as well as outside buildings
- Avoid hidden corners and inactive edges
- Consider use and perception of CCTV

section two: designing and building for… positive behaviour

Designing and building for...
community use and development

The extended schools approach strengthens the role schools can play in providing access to wider services and activities to meet the needs of their pupils, families and the wider community, including:

- a range of interesting activities before- and after-school and during the school holidays
- 8am-6pm year-round childcare
- parenting support – including family learning activities
- specialist support services
- community use of school facilities such as sport, art and ICT.

School grounds have a vital role to play in this provision in that they can provide:

- a safe, child-focused and welcoming environment that caters for the needs of all children
- a focus for community action
- a centrally-valued community resource.

Safe child-focused environment

Children and young people need the opportunity and facilities to enjoy recreational activities and informal learning within their communities. School grounds can support a number of before- and after-school activities, including after-school clubs and sports clubs. Schools may have specialist facilities to share with neighbouring schools, such as a sensory garden or a climbing wall. Garden creation projects could take place in school holidays.

Designing school grounds with and for communities will help to support children and young people of all ages. The particular needs of babies and very young children need to be considered where children's centres are located on primary school sites. Children with disabilities and special needs and those who may be visiting unfamiliar school sites will also have specific requirements that need to be factored into design, particularly around access.

Focus for community action

Adults as community stakeholders

There are a number of potential opportunities for parents and other adults to benefit directly from school grounds developments, both through the development process as well as the final product, including:

- involvement in the development, management and maintenance of the site
- access to improved facilities
- benefiting from focused projects such as nature conservation, horticulture and art
- gaining valuable skills and knowledge through voluntary work or training.

▶ **Right**
A great place to meet and discuss school grounds developments.

◢ **Below**
Local employees are often keen to get involved.

To help with this it's worth developing a whole-school policy for community partnerships and use of the site, negotiating a general agreed code of conduct for all users and formal access agreements for specific groups, which could include a trial period, and should be closely monitored and periodically reviewed.
The agreements should identify:

- the separate groups involved
- the specific nature of the use of the site, including timings for when the activities begin and end
- a clear understanding of the roles and responsibilities of the users, including any financial provision or legal implications
- consideration of ongoing management and maintenance
- penalties for not abiding by the agreement.

Points to consider:

- Potential users of the site should be helped to understand the school's values and priorities in providing for children's needs.
- Any specific activities should be negotiated and agreed by the school, based on an assessment of local resources available and accessibility of facilities.
- Caretakers and other site supervisors are the gatekeepers of the school facilities, of even greater importance when a school develops its role in the community – they must be consulted and involved in the formulation and implementation of any code of conduct or access agreements.
- A project like developing school grounds can bring parents together, both through their involvement in the process and their use of the site.
- This could perhaps be the first step towards PTA (Parent Teachers Association) membership, or eventually becoming a school governor.

section two: designing and building for… community use and development   79

Far left
A social gathering after a busy day's gardening helps create a sense of community belonging.

Left
An external amphitheatre on a sloping site links to the assembly and dining halls.

A centrally-valued community resource

Involving adults in design and development

As members of the school community, adults can add value to school grounds' developments, whether they have children at the school or not. For example:

- Consulting with the community and incorporating their needs into the site design can:

  - provide valuable opportunities to strengthen partnerships with stakeholders such as local sports clubs and community agencies (as long as these needs complement those of the children), increasing a sense of ownership and belonging

  - help to secure valuable investment for the site and raise significant revenue to offset the additional management and maintenance costs associated with the extended use of the site.

- School grounds improvement projects can be a catalyst for uniting disparate elements around a common cause, prompting relationships to develop and communities to strengthen.

- Valuable community links can be forged by drawing on individuals' expertise, linking local businesses together to provide additional investment and enlisting volunteers to carry out practical work.

- The skills and experience gained by working on school grounds improvement projects could even contribute towards vocational education for various members of the community.

All schools are different, each reflecting their communities. Linked to creating an identity and 'sense of place', school grounds designs should reflect the cultural diversity of those using the school space. Spaces can be created to support activities that might take place out of school hours – sheltered seating areas, for instance, gathering places and spaces outdoors for classes such as yoga or T'ai Chi.

The Extended Schools programme encourages schools to form partnerships with other agencies and organisations. A range of partnerships can be considered in the design process and final outcome. Some of the most common activities are described opposite.

designing school grounds

▶ **Right**
Pupils' artwork can reflect local heritage and community.

▶▶ **Far right**
This community orchard provides practical and educational opportunities.

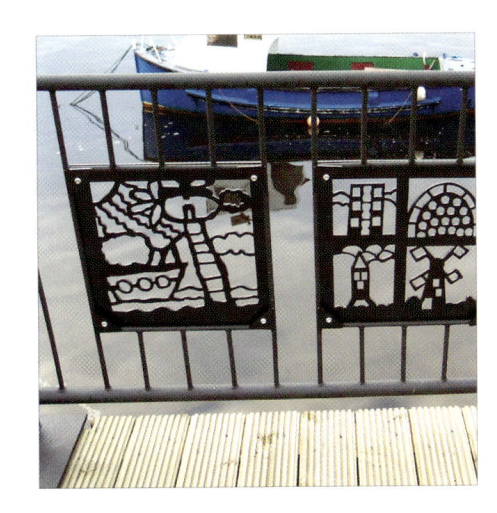

Work-related learning

For older students and other adults in the community, there is great potential to work with organisations and initiatives in the community and begin to understand how professionals work. Projects can:

- encourage links with local colleges, businesses and voluntary groups as sources of expertise and support
- be the focus for schools working as clusters, either informally or as federations
- include secondary students working with primary schools to help them improve their grounds.

Community sports

Local sports clubs provide opportunities for community partnerships, which can be supported by school sports coordinators – they have, as a key work area, building and supporting school-club links and developing out-of-hours opportunities. Local sports clubs, after-school clubs and summer play schemes may be able to part-fund improvements as well as contribute to the structured management and use of these facilities through organised coaching sessions and other supervision. These key stakeholders should be included in any consultation on developing school grounds.

The regional offices of Sport England (www.sportengland.org) and the Youth Sport Trust (www.youthsporttrust.org) can offer valuable support.

Community arts

Community arts programmes involving 'artists in residence' could be used to work with children and young people in after-school clubs to create installations and pieces of art that engage children's imaginations, reflect the context of the site, improve the aesthetics of the site and provide a tangible sense of achievement for those involved.

◀ **Left**
Parents learn how to explore the local habitat and identify wildlife.

▶ **Right**
Working with a local artist on a community arts programme engages children and adults.

◣ **Below**
A welcoming space where parents can meet and talk while dropping off and collecting children.

Growing into a wider community resource

School grounds are part of our open space resource and as such they can contribute wildlife, landscape, recreational and play value.
The grounds can offer community value in other ways, including providing recycling facilities, youth club areas or local produce areas. Designing to improve these values will add to community resources and potentially help meet other targets set in locally devised plans of action.

Groups and organisations, such as local sports clubs, local authority staff, church groups, youth organisations such as Scouts and Guides, charities, local interest groups and parent and toddler groups, can support and help to make these improvements happen by working directly with children before and after school. They should be involved as community stakeholders within the design process.

There are useful references listed in the **information sources** on page 116.

AT A GLANCE

SAFE CHILD-FOCUSED ENVIRONMENT

- Consider informal play and recreational spaces
- Consider extra-curricular activities and their audiences eg youth organisations like Guides, youth clubs, toddler groups
- Consider other community links and partners at school

COMMUNITY ACTION

- Consider multi-purpose recreational spaces
- Work with partnerships in the sports, arts, and other specialist areas
- Use local expertise, especially find out about parents' skills
- Consider practical working parties, social gatherings and celebrations
- Look at inter-generational learning
- Set up community-use agreements
- Identify management and maintenance tasks

CENTRALLY-VALUED RESOURCE

- Use the local context and add value to this open space resource
- Investigate opportunities for pupils to work with local professionals and organisations
- Establish links with other schools and colleges

Designing and building for... sustainable outcomes

Sustainability is a key concept for this century and has come to mean different things to different people.

A widely-used and accepted definition of sustainable development is *"development which meets the needs of the present without compromising the ability of future generations to meet their own needs"*.[24] It's essentially about joining up our thinking on environmental, social and economic factors.

The new DfES Sustainable Schools website (www.teachernet.gov.uk/sustainableschools), launched in June 2006, provides:

- information
- interactive tools to use to progress whole school sustainability
- case studies
- resources
- sources of advice and support.

School grounds can offer outstanding learning experiences when they're designed and used following sustainable development principles:

- adopting sustainable design and management practice
- conserving and enhancing nature
- experimenting with innovative sustainable techniques
- working together and belonging
- embedding into the curriculum and school culture.

A whole-school approach will look at culture and ethos, how the curriculum supports sustainability, how the campus reflects a sustainable ethos and how the wider community contributes to sustainability.

Sustainable design and management

What we choose to build and how we do it has a significant impact on sustainability. The construction of features outside must follow the same principles being adopted by architects and building industries.

Points to consider:

- Design for minimum environmental impact.
- Re-use materials on site and source recycled materials.
- Construct with minimum energy use.
- Design and build for the conservation of water resources.
- Use locally-sourced materials and local contractors.
- Respect locally-distinctive crafts and skills.
- Maximise the positive capacity of the natural environment, including light, shade, ventilation and micro-climate.
- Design in an integrated and holistic way.
- Make optimal use of green technologies, such as renewable energy and reed bed filtration.

Creating and linking habitats, and planning for their management, ensures better space for wildlife, and good learning opportunities.

Car Park

Possible Site for Concrete Garage or Metal Shed

Bin Store

Vegetable Garden

Water Butts to collect rainwater from roof

Compost Heaps

Shrubs to Attract Birds and Butterflies

Herbs

Pond

Bog

Stone pile

Log pile

Bark chipping Path

Fence gate

extend hedgerow

School Building

Teaching Area (close-mown grass or bark chippings with log seats / picnic tables)

Native Woodland with woodland bulbs and flowers (blue-bells, primroses, ferns, wood anemones, snowdrops)

Native Hedgerow

leave this area as undisturbed as possible to encourage wildlife

close-mown paths / clearings winding through woodland. (most grass left long - meadow areas created)

Scale 1:400

Wildlife garden: work to be carried out gradually by pupils, teachers, parents and others over the summer and autumn and beyond.

Future possibilities: timber decking extending over the edge of the pond or a bridge across it, to allow better access to the deep part of the pond for pond-dipping. Identification boards, nest boxes, bat boxes, hybernicutum, hide, squirrel-proof bird feeders.

section two: designing and building for... sustainable outcomes

◄◄ Far left
Wildflower boundaries provide a wildlife habitat and also add colour and interest.

◄ Middle left
Bird-feeding stations, hedgehog houses, bee and bat boxes – their location is important.

◄ Left
Spaces throughout the grounds can build up nectar sources for bees and butterflies.

Conserving and enhancing nature

- Include ongoing maintenance in project management systems to ensure long-term quality.
- Build in responsibility for the design and its implementation to create ownership and understanding.
- It's worth setting up a school grounds project group, school council or steering group to help establish a sustainable management process across the whole school.
- Whole-site developments can be expensive but worth every penny.
- It's crucial to plan over the long-term so that unexpected opportunities can be taken advantage of in a sustainable way, in keeping with the overall design.
- High-quality items and outcomes last longer and remain in good condition.
- Finances need to be planned to allow for the continued and sustainable evolution of the outside space.

School grounds can provide diverse habitats for plants and animals, even in the smallest of sites – it's even possible to create a nature reserve. Before anything else is done in the grounds there needs to be a habitat, vegetation and wildlife survey. Strong bold elements can be included in new designs, which both conserve and enhance this biodiversity.

Points to consider:

- Existing habitat features such as hedgerows, grassland, woodlands and individual trees can be enhanced through positive management and additions. New habitats can be created – the type will be influenced by local conditions. Local Biodiversity Action Plans[25] provide information on local habitats and individual species with their conservation priorities.
- Areas of perennial rye grass can be transformed into meadow habitat – either on a large scale or as borders adjacent to other habitats such as hedges, through meadow creation using seed, seed mats or plug planting. It's important to plan how these are going to be maintained.
- Local wildlife advice should guide the types of new habitat creation in school grounds, according to what's most appropriate.
- The choice of plants to use and the method used to create the habitat are crucial to success. When you're creating new wildlife habitat it's good practice to use lists of local plants and to echo naturally occurring groups of plants.
- Provide an opportunity to investigate natural succession in undisturbed areas, as well as designing places where wildlife can be allowed to have sanctuary. In larger school grounds this is very possible and can add significantly to biodiversity.
- Organic and locally-produced fruit and vegetables from schools are adding to the local food movement and our renewed connection with local environment and heritage.

▶ **Right**
Using children's artwork in signage and other features adds a creative touch.

◀ **Below**
Sedum roofs on outdoor buildings add vegetation, improve insulation and demonstrate new design ideas.

Experimenting with innovative sustainable techniques

Learning about environmental management and sustainability is crucial to our future thinking and requires hands-on opportunities.

Points to consider:

- School grounds can provide opportunities to:
  - devise and build technological solutions for developing alternative energy systems
  - experiment and build with recycled materials
  - use organic products and practise organic gardening.

- By providing good facilities such as secure cycle sheds and well-designed access routes, school grounds can also promote sustainable transport – cycling and walking – and should be a consideration within School Travel Plans[26].

- A life-cycle analysis of materials used, with cost benefit analysis, could be an integral part of the design brief, offering many opportunities to learn about sustainability issues.

section two: designing and building for… sustainable outcomes

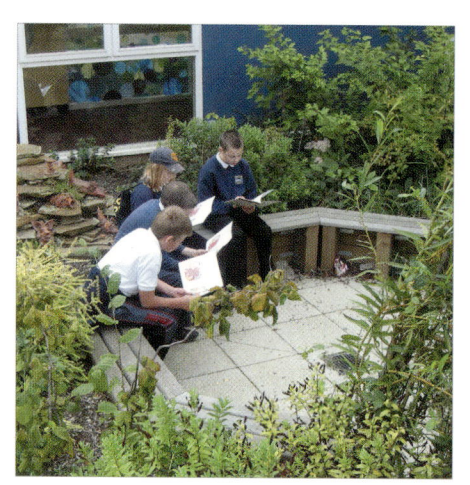

◀ **Left**
Interlinked features and spaces work well for teaching and building a sense of place.

▶ **Below**
This primary school's bird hide takes advantage of fields and hedgerows beyond the school boundary, linking in to newly 'diversified' meadowland and incorporating teaching elements.

Working together and belonging

Changes and developments in school ground have significant potential for becoming models of sustainability, laying the foundations for a sustainable mindset.

Active participation grows a culture of positive thinking and self value, and will help to ensure that the development process itself is sustainable, with ownership and responsibility being passed among pupils and staff.
The ethos of providing time and space for creativity and innovation permeates the school's curriculum and its culture. Outdoor spaces are a valuable opportunity for inspiration.

Points to consider:

- Designing for sustainability should reflect local distinctiveness. This could translate into the materials used, the themes developed, the dominant shapes and designs.
- Use the new design to enhance a sense of belonging to the community.

PLANNING FOR THE FUTURE – CLIMATE CHANGE

Climate change can no longer be ignored and should be considered in all school grounds decisions. This means:

- Planning for a drier climate, hotter summers and potentially wetter warmer winters.
- Using plants that best suit these conditions – drought-resistant (often low-maintenance).
- Thinking about water table changes and how to innovate to help collect much-needed water for growing plants.
- Planning bog gardens and ponds to take advantage of retaining water.
- Using sheltered south facing walls for Mediterranean-type vegetation.

88 designing school grounds

Embedding

Sustainability within a school will mean that the outdoor space is a rich and unbeatable curriculum resource. Embedding the use of the outdoor space into the school's curriculum, into development plans, schemes of work and daily use will ensure the space is continuously used, developed, adapted and maintained. See the **designing for teaching and learning** section for more information.

AT A GLANCE

PRINCIPLES

DESIGN AND MANAGEMENT

- Use environmental principles
- Recycle and re-use
- Source ethical materials
- Use local contractors and designers
- Work to environmental attributes
- Make use of existing groups, such as school councils, or set up specific teams, such as a school grounds steering or management group
- Implement a project management system
- Set aside budget
- Consider quality of materials

CONSERVING AND ENHANCING NATURE

- Carry out wildlife surveys
- Plan in habitat management
- Consider habitat creation and enhancement including wildlife strips and borders
- Allow succession
- Make habitat connections and adopt less intensive regimes, such as grass mowing
- Set up larger sanctuaries if possible

WORKING TOGETHER

- Reflect cultural diversity and school identity
- Respect and build on local distinctiveness
- Plan in community involvement

EMBEDDING

- Create practical outdoor teaching spaces – read more in the **designing and building for learning and teaching** section
- Write school policies and schemes of work relating to school grounds

MORE IDEAS

SUSTAINABLE PRACTICE

- Solar panels
- Wind turbines
- Reed bed filtration
- Permaculture
- Shelter belts
- Use of grey water
- Roof gardens
- Energy coppice
- Cycling facilities
- Compost bins
- Water butts
- Drought-resistant planting
- Traditional crafts, such as hedge laying

Designing and building for... different sectors and needs

Early years

The general themes considered in the previous pages apply to all sites. But different educational sectors also have specific needs that need to be considered when the outdoor space is being designed. Where a site is used by several age groups, it's important to consider how these disparate needs can be integrated.

Designing outdoor spaces for very young children requires a different approach than for older children, not least because the curriculum guidance for the Foundation Stage explicitly sets out children's entitlement to outdoor play[27].

Research over many years has shown that young children need movement and activity[28] to help them make the neural connections that allow the brain to learn. In the main, children learn by doing – this is especially true for boys. A well-designed outdoor space can not only cater for this type of learning, but will also allow children to engage in quiet, reflective play and many other activities, without compromising others' enjoyment of the space.

Every early years setting is unique, with its own special space, staff, children and parents. But some rules of thumb can be applied to the design of outdoor spaces[29] for these settings, as long as they are used in the context of each setting's specific needs. It's perfectly possible for very young children to participate in the decision-making process – as with older children; they are, after all, the 'experts' in their own environment. Several approaches have been developed with young children in mind[30], including using props to encourage dialogue, and taking photographs or otherwise marking out special places.

Points to consider:

- There should be a balance of hard and soft landscaping, including hard surfaces, grass, planting, trees, sand and safer surfacing.

- Managed risk and challenge are vital to young children's development. The space should allow children to safely challenge themselves, to grow and to experiment. This needn't necessarily mean fixed climbing equipment. Simple structures to allow activities such as stepping, balancing and climbing are equally valuable.

▶ **Right**
Awnings, shutters and blinds allow transitional space to be open or enclosed.

◀ **Far right and below**
A flexible and imaginative approach makes even small spaces continually interesting.

- Shelter and shade are important – created through planting or fixed features such as playhouses, for example. Providing some means of attaching a temporary shelter to an external wall can make a space more adaptable – such as fixing hooks for fastening a sail, or building a pergola that could be draped with fabric.

- A transitional space should be provided next to the exit to the outdoors, to allow children (and adults) to see the outdoors and the activities taking place there before making decisions about joining in. In many settings this space is covered, thereby extending the 'indoors' whilst providing shelter and fresh air.

- Changes in topography and levels, a variety of textures, colours and shapes, all contribute to a successful outdoor play space.

- If outdoor space isn't currently accessible, there may need to be a review of the arrangement of outdoor and indoor spaces so that early years can occupy an internal space with direct access to outside.

- In a school situation, the relationship between outdoor spaces used by early years and those used by older children may be important in terms of integration and transition. Avoiding duplication of resources and ensuring safety of all children is also important.

- Security and access need to be considered when an appropriate space is being identified. For example, parents, often with prams, will want to wait close by when they're collecting children.

- It's important that some space remain free of features or planned activities. Exploration is key to young children's learning outdoors and a high-quality space will include plenty of opportunities for children to invent their own play, using found or supplied resources.

- Staff will want to adapt the space to suit current or future themes, or to build upon and extend children's current interests.

section two: designing and building for… different sectors and needs   91

◀ **Left**
Children's artwork adds interest and colour.

▼ **Below**
The children helped design and create this environmental artwork and will learn about photosynthesis as the grass returns to green.

92　designing school grounds

Right and below
Using features in the school grounds to explain maths concepts in a practical, meaningful way.

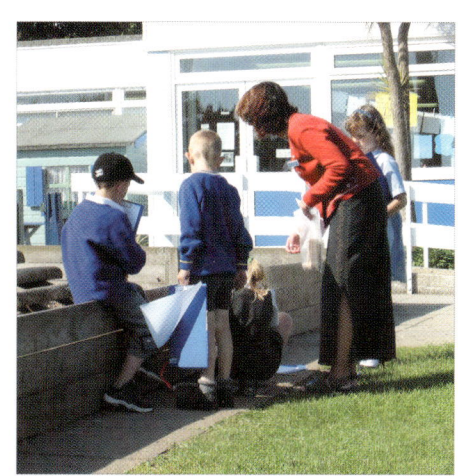

Primary

Successful primary school playgrounds cater for children's play needs by age, gender and individual preference – but this can be a challenging task. At 5 years old, a child's outdoor play needs are very different from those of an 11 year old. Formal curriculum requirements also make demands on the space. See section two, **developing school grounds**, for more insight.

School grounds development projects in primary schools lend themselves to an holistic approach because many of the activities associated with change can be linked to the curriculum. What's more, children are still very interested in 'play' and feel a close bond with their school.

Involving primary school pupils is generally a simpler task than at secondary level or with very young children – they are old enough to begin to understand more sophisticated planning concepts, yet young enough to be enthusiastic and motivated about the project.

Points to consider:

- Appeal to children's intellect and sense of fun with features designed to stimulate their senses and encourage physical and mental exploration.

- Have a variety of seating options – in several areas, in different arrangements and locations – to allow a range of social and teaching groupings to take place.

- Ongoing management policies should encourage and allow pupils and staff to adapt the space and its uses to suit current and future priorities.

- 'Open-ended' playground markings allow a wide variety of uses but don't dominate the space.

- Opportunities for physical activity, both formal (PESS, sports clubs) and informal (active play), should be given appropriate space so that children can develop and extend skills.

- Community use should build upon and strengthen the school's position at the heart of the community.

section two: designing and building for… different sectors and needs   93

◀ Left
'Play' is as important for older pupils as it is for younger.

▼ Below
A wind turbine and solar-powered river system provide practical learning opportunities.

"By providing spaces for students to sit, chat and eat their lunch, there are now more visible role-models of good behaviour, which has had a socialising effect."

Deputy Headteacher, secondary school

Secondary

Research[31] by the National Foundation for Educational Research and Learning through Landscapes shows that:

- The nature and quality of the outdoor school environment matters deeply to students of secondary school age.
- There are educational, social, aesthetic, environmental and community arguments for improving secondary school grounds.
- The process of helping to plan and implement school grounds improvements can be deeply beneficial in terms of student learning and self-confidence, and staff development.
- A better outdoor school environment can lead to positive changes in students' attitudes and new resources for curriculum teaching and learning.

School grounds development projects can provide great opportunities for secondary schools and their pupils, including:

Citizenship in action
The process of planning developments to the school grounds provides real experience of citizenship skills. Read more in **section one**. Links can also be made across the curriculum through student involvement in researching and designing changes, gathering opinions and managing budgets.

Meeting the needs of the 14-19 curriculum
School grounds can be a useful resource for delivering vocational courses as part of the 14-19 curriculum. On-site practical work for NVQs and BTECs in subjects such as Horticulture or Land and Environment provide valuable learning experiences for students — and improve the grounds for the whole school. It may also be possible to transfer tasks to students as part of their coursework.

Promoting positive behaviour and well-being
The poor behaviour at breaktime that concerns many secondary schools is often due to a lack of recreational and social opportunities and the territorial conflicts generated by inadequate school grounds design.

▶ **Right**
Students learn about horticulture and develop business skills in the allotments and market gardens within these school grounds.

▶▶ **Far right**
Sitting in a circle makes conversation easier.

Points to consider:

- **Socialising** – important for all young people, and one way that they 'play', a need often overlooked at secondary level. In many secondary schools there's a lack of comfortable, well-designed spaces for socialising and eating outdoors, spaces that are sheltered and fully furnished with features such as seating that young people say they most need. Providing such spaces designed specifically to meet the needs of young people can improve breaktime behaviour and discourage students from leaving the school during lunchtime, thus avoiding a source of conflict with the local community. It can also provide outdoor teaching areas and spaces to meet or gather at the start or end of the school day. These social spaces need to support different age groups and genders.

- **Physical activity** – secondary school grounds often cater only for traditional sports, such as football and basketball. Exploring the activities that students choose to take part in outside school may help to identify changes that can be made to the school grounds to encourage more active lifestyles. It's important that such changes are designed to be suitable for this age group – activity trails can be popular with teenagers, for example, but not if they are too small and insufficiently challenging.

- **The needs of different groups** – playtime is fun in primary schools but Year 7 pupils leave a school environment in July which supports and encourages fun and go to another in September where there's often little to do during breaktimes except "hang around" and try to "keep out of trouble". More often than not teenage pupils see 'play' as being childish, although sports are deemed acceptable.

- **Grounds designed for informal use** – these need to reflect the age range of the pupils. The older students may lean towards a more adult 'campus style' environment, while children who have just arrived from primary school may want a 'safer' more contained space, where they can 'play'.

- **Girls and boys are likely to have disparate needs** – as well as individual preferences for activities, there may be differences in the sizes of social groups that will need to be reflected in the arrangement of seating.

◀ **Left**
Planters enable those with mobility problems to tend plants.

◤ **Below**
The detailed design of ordinary features can make a significant difference – such as the sensory tiles on this gate.

◤ **Bottom**
A sensory pergola encourages pupils to use all their senses.

Special Educational Needs

It is important to consider the needs of all children in the design of school grounds and to ensure that provision is made to cater for children with disabilities and Special Educational Needs, taking account of the varying needs pupils may have.

This applies to all school sites, whether mainstream, special or campus sites, where special schools or units share facilities with a mainstream school.

Special schools cater for pupils with behavioural problems, physical difficulties, learning difficulties or a mixture of needs. Some specialise in catering for children with specific needs, such as those with an autistic spectrum disorder or sensory impairment. The age range of special schools can be much wider than in the mainstream, and some schools are residential. Some share their outside space, so consideration should be given to the similar and contrasting needs of the different user groups. Features and activities designed for pupils with special educational needs, such as sensory gardens, can be just as valuable to pupils who don't have these needs.

It's vital when you're developing existing grounds to look at current use – and talk to staff and pupils about potential future use to find out the particular needs of the school.

There's specific information and guidance for special school grounds development in *Building Bulletin 77*[32] and *Grounds for Sharing*[33].

Points to consider:

- **Access** – There are likely to be pupils with specific access requirements in most special schools. Some will use wheelchairs; others will be semi-ambulant; others visually impaired. Each of these has particular access needs, the solutions to which provide opportunities to develop skills and increase confidence in pupils. All pupils need to be able to access as much of the grounds as possible, although some areas may provide more of a challenge for pupils to reach and use:

96 designing school grounds

▶ **Right**
Social areas are particularly important for children with special educational needs.

▶▶ **Far right**
Gardening is known to have valuable therapeutic qualities.

◀ **Below**
Many pupils with special needs enjoy physical aspects of learning – and develop transferable skills.

- sports courts and their surroundings may need adapting to allow for variations of rules. There should also be other non-sporting elements that challenge and stretch pupils physically, such as pathways with different surfaces or obstacle and adventure courses

- a number of pupils may need regular physiotherapy and creating secluded and sheltered spaces for this would enable them to come outside more often.

- **Sensory experiences** – many special schools have a sensory room inside, elements of which could be developed further in the grounds. A separate sensory area might be provided outside but sensory elements can also be built into the overall design of the grounds – such as paths with different textures, planting with changing colours or scents, tactile signage, moving sculptures or musical elements.

- **Social skills** – there may be a wide range of social needs to be met within one school. Different styles and sizes of social spaces can cater for different abilities, preferences and ages. Play can also help with the development of social skills and there needs to be provision for creative, cognitive, physical and social play within the grounds.

- **Learning outdoors** – many children with special needs benefit from learning through doing. Providing them with opportunities to undertake practical activities outside can be of particular benefit and teachers often say that many pupils thrive when lessons are taken outside.

- **Preparing for life outside school** – for children with special needs, preparing for life outside school is a vital part of their schooling. This might include specialist work skills as well as general social, educational and mobility skills. Horticulture and construction skills are among those regularly taught and these can be supported by appropriate provision in the grounds.

section two: designing and building for... different sectors and needs

& flowers

section **three**

**supporting
school grounds
development**

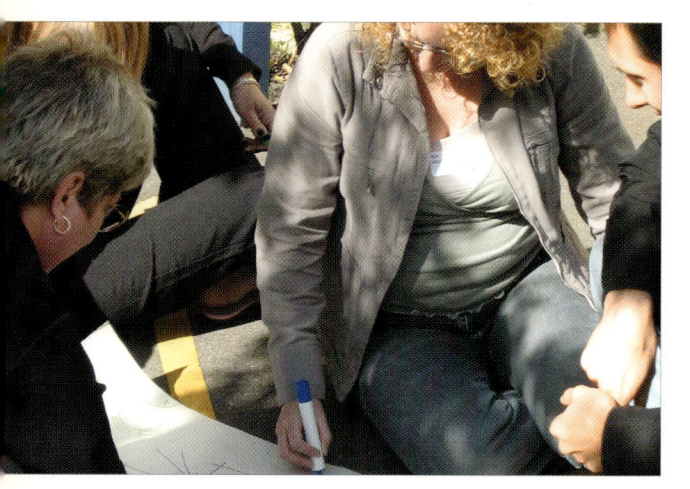

Left
School staff sharing ideas with the designer.

Below
School grounds professionals attending further training with Learning through Landscapes.

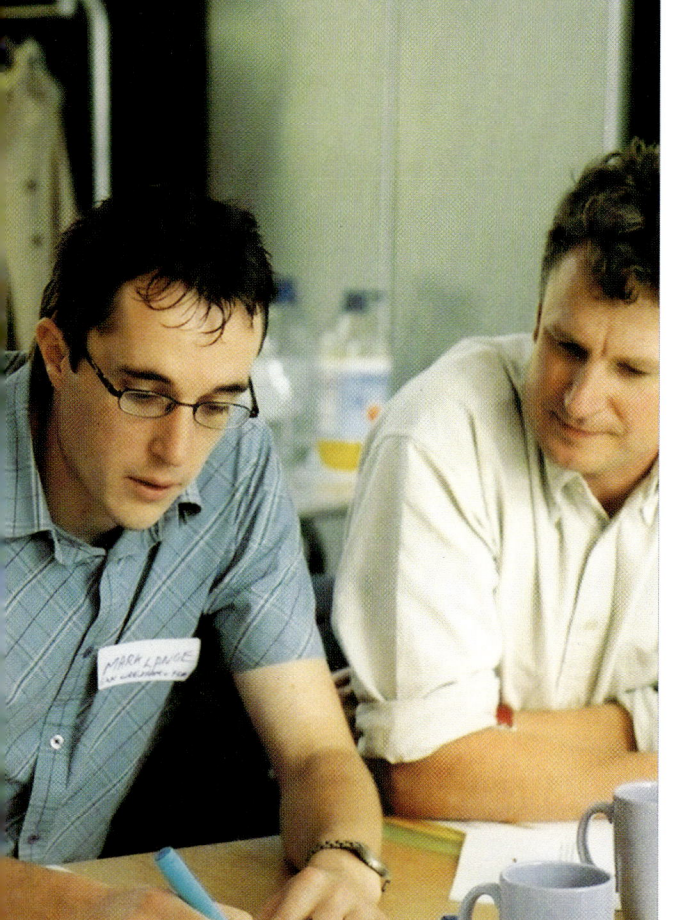

Who can help?

Why get help to develop the grounds?

Having specialist skills support will help schools make informed decisions about their outdoor spaces, offering perspectives that are likely to add value to the school's planning for outdoor learning and play. From a design professional's point of view, schools themselves – the pupils, staff and wider community – can offer critical information and unique insights into the potential of school grounds. And that's vital for successful design.

What type of support is available?

Learning through Landscapes (LTL), the national school grounds charity, has coined the phrase 'school grounds professional' to help identify individuals and organisations with appropriate knowledge and skills and the capacity to support schools in the development of their grounds. LTL operates an accredited training and facilitation scheme, supported by professional membership to school grounds professionals throughout the country.

▶ **Right**
Preparatory work carried out by students and their surveyor.

◢ **Below**
Carefully designed shady pathway at a Cornish primary school.

▶▶ **Far right**
Volunteers work with pupils to build a new pathway.

Points to consider:

- The term 'school grounds professional' encompasses a diverse range of occupations, including design professionals, educators and workers in the play sector.

- Very often, a school grounds professional has a number of skills – for example, a bespoke play equipment supplier might also be a sculptor, or a landscape architect might also provide specialist training or facilitation, or be a project manager.

- As well as professional support, schools should always look to their school community and beyond for skilled and unskilled help. A skills audit of the parents may well identify potential volunteers (or professionals who might be contracted) to work on the project.

- Smaller scale projects often rely on parents and the community to carry out the work – for example clearing, digging, planting, making, painting playground markings or perhaps producing informal seating or landscape features.

- Volunteer teams are often available through, for example, British Trust for Conservation Volunteers (BTCV) and Groundwork. Sport England and the Youth Sports Trust provide valuable advice on school sport. See the **where to find external support** section at the end of this chapter.

- To get the best from a school grounds professional, the whole school community must be ready to get properly involved in the debate and decision making. Before external experts are invited in, it's important that the 'real' experts – the school's stakeholders – are aware of what's happening.

- Once the need for a particular skill has been established, it's helpful to set broad targets or performance indicators for the outcomes of the piece of work, such as successful implementation, regular use, or increased learning opportunities.

section three: supporting school grounds development

WHAT COULD THEY HELP WITH?

- ● Very likely to be able to help
- ● May be able to help

WHO CAN HELP?			Design issues	Construction advice	Materials	Equipment	Planting	Surfaces and features	Project management	Policies and management	Using the grounds	Curriculum support	Planning	Participation	Fundraising	Sustainability issues	Labour/construction
	Design	Landscape architect	●	●	●	●	●	●	●	●			●	●	●	●	
		Garden designer	●	●	●		●	●			●				●		●
		Surveyor		●	●			●	●				●				
		Artist/sculptor	●	●	●			●	●			●		●	●		●
		Contractor	●	●	●	●	●	●	●							●	●
	Educators	Trainer							●	●	●			●		●	
		Facilitator	●						●	●	●	●	●	●	●	●	
		Wildlife adviser	●	●	●		●		●	●	●	●				●	●
		Environmental /sustainability adviser	●					●		●	●	●	●			●	
	Play	Play consultant	●			●		●	●	●	●		●		●		
		Playworker				●				●	●	●		●			
		Playground equipment supplier	●	●	●	●		●	●						●		●
	Other	Fundraiser							●	●			●		●		
		Project manager	●	●	●	●	●	●	●				●		●	●	
		Parents /community			●		●				●			●	●		●

102 designing school grounds

What sort of help is needed?

The earlier section on **developing school grounds** should help schools establish what they need in terms of the use, design and management of their school grounds. This will make it easier to decide on the sort of external support they need. Some general examples are outlined below – specific needs should be talked through with professionals before agreeing a contract with them. The relevance of support will also depend on the scope of the development, such as whether it's an existing or new site.

Points to consider:

- When you're using volunteer or unskilled labour to complete a project on school grounds, make sure they adhere to health and safety regulations.
- Carry out a risk assessment of each task, ensure volunteers are fully briefed, and supervise the task throughout.
- See **designing and building for healthy lifestyles** for more information about risk and challenge, and risk assessments.

Adding value

School grounds professionals can add enormous value to a school grounds project in a number of ways:

- **Design professionals** – are experts in their field. But there's more to design than simply creating a solution to meet a brief. A good designer will create a unique and interesting space, which challenges and entices its users and provides logical circulation and communication systems.

- **Educators (trainers or facilitators)** – can help teaching and non-teaching staff consider the formal, informal and 'hidden' curriculum implications of improvements to the school grounds, offering on-site support to help schools make the most of their grounds for learning and teaching, for play and for informal or extra-curricular use.

- **Playworkers** – it's worth schools considering bringing in a playworker or consultant to provide a specialist perspective on informal or extra-curricular use of the grounds – especially important for extended schools. A play consultant may offer play training for staff or work directly with children and could help with creating and implementing playground or behaviour management policies.

- **Community members (including parents)** – not only are there often specialist skills available; but using volunteers rather than paid labour can make the difference between being able to implement a project in full and having to cut corners. Remember that volunteer labour can usually be included as a gift in kind on grant and award application forms.

- **Fundraisers or project managers** – come from various backgrounds and are likely to have many other skills such as landscape design or environmental management.

Choosing a school grounds professional: questions to ask

- **Do we feel we could get on with this person?** Do they appreciate and understand the ethos of the school? Are they listening carefully and respecting opinions? Can they apply their knowledge and skills to the specific situation?

- **What are the expected outcomes for this piece of work?** Should there be performance indicators or other measurement tools? How will the work be monitored and evaluated? What comeback will there be if the outcomes are not satisfactory?

- **What experience of working with children of the relevant ages does this school grounds professional have?** How will they ensure the children are able to participate meaningfully? Can they provide references or names of schools they have previously worked with?

- **Do they charge for their services?** If so, how much? A daily rate or a fixed fee? How frequently will they invoice?

Where to find external support

These are just some of the organisations that may be able to provide help and support for a school grounds development. It's also worth scanning local directories.

Learning through Landscapes (LTL)
www.ltl.org.uk
LTL operates a members' advice line, where members can discuss school grounds improvements and be put in touch with school grounds professionals in their area, many of whom are accredited by LTL as trainers or facilitators. These professionals are supported by a tailored professional membership package. LTL also provides training and has a range of publications relating to the design, use and management of school grounds. A Who Can Help? advice sheet is also available, with case studies and examples of good practice.

Arts Council of England
www.arts.org.uk
The Arts Council has regional offices, which can help with local artists.

Axis
www.axisartists.org.uk
An arts organisation listing artists in a searchable database.

BTCV
www.btcv.org.uk
A number of local BTCV offices provide a specialised support service for schools that want to undertake conservation projects.

Groundwork UK
www.groundwork.org.uk
Groundwork operates a network of trusts around the country and may be able to provide professional services to schools that want to improve their grounds, including using volunteer teams to implement projects.

Growing Schools
www.teachernet.gov.uk/growingschools
Growing Schools encourages schools to use the outdoors as a resource across the curriculum for pupils of all ages and abilities. The website is designed to provide a one-stop-shop, with a huge directory of resources, case studies, research and sources of support.

The Landscape Institute
www.l-i.org.uk
Lists all registered landscape architects.

Local authorities
Local authorities usually employ landscape architects and surveyors and whilst every local authority is different, these professionals are likely to be found within a department such as Environment, Planning, Property Services, Estates, Leisure Services or Regeneration.

National Playing Fields Association (NPFA)
www.npfa.org
The national organisation with specific responsibility for acquiring, protecting and improving playing fields and playgrounds. See website or call 020 7833 5360 (Head Office).

RICS
www.rics.org.uk
Look for a surveyor on their website.

Royal Society for the Prevention of Accidents (RoSPA)
www.rospa.org.uk
A national organisation aiming to campaign for change, influence opinion, contribute to debate and educate and inform. RoSPA is actively involved in the promotion and the prevention of accidents in all areas of life – at work, in the home, and on the roads, in schools, at leisure and on (or near) water. See website or call 0121 248 2000.

Society of Garden Designers
www.sgd.org.uk

Sport England
www.sportengland.org
Sport England deliver the Government's sporting objectives. They provide valuable guidance documents and support through their regional offices.

Thrive
www.thrive.org.uk
Thrive is a national charity whose aim is to enable positive change in the lives of disabled and disadvantaged people through the use of gardening and horticulture. Thrive offers training and resources and can help schools ensure that pupils with special needs can make the most of school grounds.

Wildlife Trusts
www.wildlifetrusts.org
The network of Wildlife Trusts runs reserves and offers educational support to schools. They will be an important port of call for advice for many projects.

Youth Sport Trust
www.youthsporttrust.org
The Youth Sport Trust works with a range of partners to deliver high quality PE and sport to all young people, regardless of ability. Their TOP programmes support toddlers to 18 year olds.

Funding

This section looks at the funding that's available for school grounds projects, giving some general advice on how to create a fundraising strategy and make an effective application for bidding pots.

Sources of funding

There are many sources of funding for school grounds development, some from the Government, some from charities and some from the private sector.

Points to consider:

- Investment in school grounds can be prioritised from capital or revenue funding programmes where schools and authorities have autonomy on their allocations.

- Where special funding is available, there's considerable variation in the complexity of application processes and the requirements of the funding bodies.

- Some funding is intended particularly for schools, while some is aimed at community groups – the Neighbourhood Renewal Fund[34] for instance – where you will need to identify the benefits of the project to the local community. Some funds can be used for both buildings and grounds, while others are specific to external spaces.

Government funding

- Information about local government funding is on the websites of the Department for Communities and Local Government (DCLG)[35] and of local authorities.

- Many local authorities have external funding officers who can offer advice and guidance.

- All local authorities receive substantial capital funding – allocated by formula according to relative need – to address their local schools investment needs as prioritised through their Asset Management Plans (AMP). These funding programmes include:
  - **modernisation** – allocated according to relative building need
  - **basic need** – to support the provision of statutory school places
  - **school access** – to support provision to meet the requirements of the Disability Discrimination Act 1995.

- Local authorities have autonomy on the use of these major funding programmes – schools can apply to them for funding.

- Local authorities may also have additional capital funds, including from planning gains or asset disposal. Arrangements for accessing these funds vary locally.

- Every school also receives direct funding – Devolved Formula Capital (DFC) – which is allocated on a per-school and per-pupil formula. Schools have autonomy on the use of DFC but are expected to invest in the priorities of the local AMP in consultation with the LEA. This funding can be rolled over for up to three years to allow larger projects to be tackled, and can also be used as matched funding or joined up with funding contributions from local authorities or other sources.

- In 2007-08, a typical secondary school will receive £113,000 and a typical primary school, £34,000. See www.teachernet.gov.uk/schoolscapital

Government funding continued...

There are also a number of funding streams specifically related to Government initiatives. The key current funding programmes can be used for both buildings and school grounds.

- **Building Schools for the Future**: aims to renew all secondary schools in England in 15 'waves'. All authorities will benefit by 2011 from inclusion in the programme, or from an early offer which will renew their neediest secondary school. See www.bsf.gov.uk
- **Primary funding**: additional capital investment available from 2008-09 to rebuild, refurbish or upgrade all primary schools to offer 21st-century learning environments. See www.teachernet.gov.uk/schoolscapital

- **The Academies programme**: enables sponsors from the private, faith and voluntary sectors to replace failing schools with new all-ability secondary schools whose running costs are met by the state. See www.standards.dfes.gov.uk/academies
- **The Targeted Capital Fund (TCF)**: supports worthwhile strategic projects that meet ministerial priorities and which might not otherwise be funded. Authorities are invited to apply for funding every two years. See www.teachernet.gov.uk/schoolscapital

- **Specialist Schools**: a one-off capital grant (which has to be match funded) available to secondary schools when they are awarded specialist status. Schools have to demonstrate how the wider community and non-specialist schools might benefit from access to the new provision. See www.standards.dfes.gov.uk/specialistschools/
- **Extended Schools**: to support, for example, breakfast clubs, family learning and adult education. See www.teachernet.gov.uk/wholeschool/extendedschools Some of these services may also be provided by Children's Centres on school sites. See www.surestart.gov.uk

Lottery funding

A wide range of projects based on good causes, including arts, heritage, sport and community, are funded through the various strands of the **national lottery**. There's information about each of these sources, including case studies about successful applications, at www.lotterygoodcauses.org.uk

Pros
- variety of pots of money available
- large sums available
- regional officers to aid process
- charitable status not always essential
- mostly good guidance notes, pre-application forms and consultation
- few deadlines
- transparent and accessible
- quick, easy access for smaller sums

Cons
- which stream should you apply for?
- overall pot getting smaller
- increased competition for funds
- lengthy application process
- application forms can be prescriptive and limiting
- jargon, replication and hoops!
- often requires match funding
- won't fund core costs

Grant-making trusts

There are around 8,500 grant-making trusts offering funding in the UK. But 90% of the funding is granted by the top 100 of these. Depending on the scale of the project, it may be worth investing in one of the many searchable databases, available on CD-ROM or online, that list charitable trusts. Alternatively, local authority funding advice workers may provide access to similar search facilities, as well as guidance on applications and strategies. Other sources of funding information are provided by organisations such as the Directory of Social Change, the Charities Aid Foundation and the Charities Information Bureau.

Pros
- lots of money available
- specific geographical areas
- ability to build a relationship
- often no set application form
- not as bureaucratic
- long-term funding possible
- funding for less topical causes
- publicity not usually required*

Cons
- often very specific criteria
- some don't fully list criteria
- lack of feedback
- driven by interests of trustees/board
- can be hidden/hard to find
- often like to fund outcomes, not costs

*This may be considered a 'con' depending on circumstance

Other sources

The private sector also often provides funding, or contributions in kind, on a local, regional or national scale.

- These funds may be available directly or through partner non-governmental organisations (NGOs), such as Learning through Landscapes, as part of a managed programme.
- There may be publicity or branding requirements associated with such funding, depending on the level of company support, and this should be taken into consideration.
- NGOs also administer programmes, often with funding attached, on behalf of the Government, the lottery and grant-making trusts.
- Income can also be generated from other users, and this can help to pay for ongoing development, management and maintenance costs.
- Schools can raise money locally, perhaps with the help of bodies such as the Parent Teacher Association.
- Parent contacts can often be very useful in approaching local charities.
- Schools can often get help in kind, most usually in terms of free advice and time from parents, though sometimes materials and use of equipment may be available.
- Schools can't borrow without the express permission of the Secretary of State, and guidance is available through www.teachernet.gov.uk/schoolscapital However, guidance includes strict terms and conditions, and in practice this permission has never been given.

Accessing funds

Creating a fundraising strategy

A focused strategy, aligned closely with the aims and objectives of the overall project, will help the project management team to think of creative ways to access a wide range of funding sources and avoid being 'funding led'. It's worth thinking about whether the local community can make use of the planned features or facilities – this is likely to appeal to many funders.

Points to consider:

- An effective fundraising strategy should:
  - determine the project's likely funding needs
  - plan how these will be met
  - identify sustainable sources of income for the continued management and maintenance of the development.
- Dividing the overall grounds development plan into a series of 'projects' that can be undertaken individually or batched together for larger funding applications will allow the most flexibility within the fundraising strategy.
- Generally, the larger the grant, the more complex and demanding the application process is. There may also be greater demands on monitoring and evaluation of process, outcomes and outputs.
- Sources of larger amounts of funding may require applicants to have charitable status, a constitution and stated aims and objectives. The Charity Commission for England and Wales[36] supplies guidance on registering as a charity as well as a sample constitution and other useful documents.
- Fundraising efforts should be prioritised to raise money for the things that are needed first – the timetable needs to be geared to the response time of each fundraising method.
- Volunteer labour should be costed into the overall project budget – the Annual Survey of Hours and Earnings (ASHE)[37], available from the Office of National Statistics, is a useful tool for calculating the value of the labour and skills offered.

Funding applications

Too many bidders fall at the first hurdle through not reading application information properly or by failing to provide the information requested – so it's important to allow plenty of time to prepare funding applications.

Feedback from major funders suggests that many bids are rejected because they:

- don't align elements of their proposal with the funder's aims
- fail to explain the need for their project and how this was identified
- don't answer all the questions on the form
- fail to meet the funder's deadline
- submit illegible/poorly written applications
- do not include requested documents (such as proof of charitable status, annual report or accounts)
- provide an inadequate budget with unrealistic costings.

Points to consider:

- Projects with a defined start and end, clearly identified needs and measurable outcomes are likely to be the most attractive to funders.
- Being able to demonstrate a good track record is also useful for securing larger awards for bigger projects later.
- When you're making individual requests to local organisations and businesses, consider the project from their perspective and adjust the approach accordingly.
  - What is it about the project and its aims that will appeal to them?
  - How will supporting the cause actually benefit them as a funder?
- When you receive support:
  - acknowledge it
  - tell them about local ownership created
  - keep them informed of the progress of the project. They may provide repeat or continued funding.

The cost of fundraising

Weigh the cost of applying to particular funding sources against the benefit that will be received if you're successful:

- Donations can mostly be used in any way and seldom require any form-filling, monitoring or evaluation – just thanks.
- Applying for statutory funding requires a far greater investment in terms of the application process, monitoring and evaluation.
- Grant-making trusts can fit anywhere along this scale – there's such variation in their requirements.
- There may be other implications of applying to particular funding sources:
  - Will a relationship with the funder affect the overall aims of the project?
  - Is it desirable to be associated with this particular funder?
  - Will establishing a relationship with a funder limit the ability to apply to others who may be seen as 'competition'?

AT A GLANCE

- Assembling the funding for an investment project may be complex and time-consuming
- Schools with investment projects for their grounds should look first to their DFC, and then to their local authority
- If these sources do not meet their needs, they will need to consider whether the shortfall is most likely to be met from local fundraising, or from application to a funding body – or from both
- As a rule of thumb, the fewer the sources of funding, the easier to manage, as some sources may be conditional on assembling the whole package
- It's also generally best if the school can show it's putting in some of its own money or locally-raised contributions

section three: supporting school grounds development

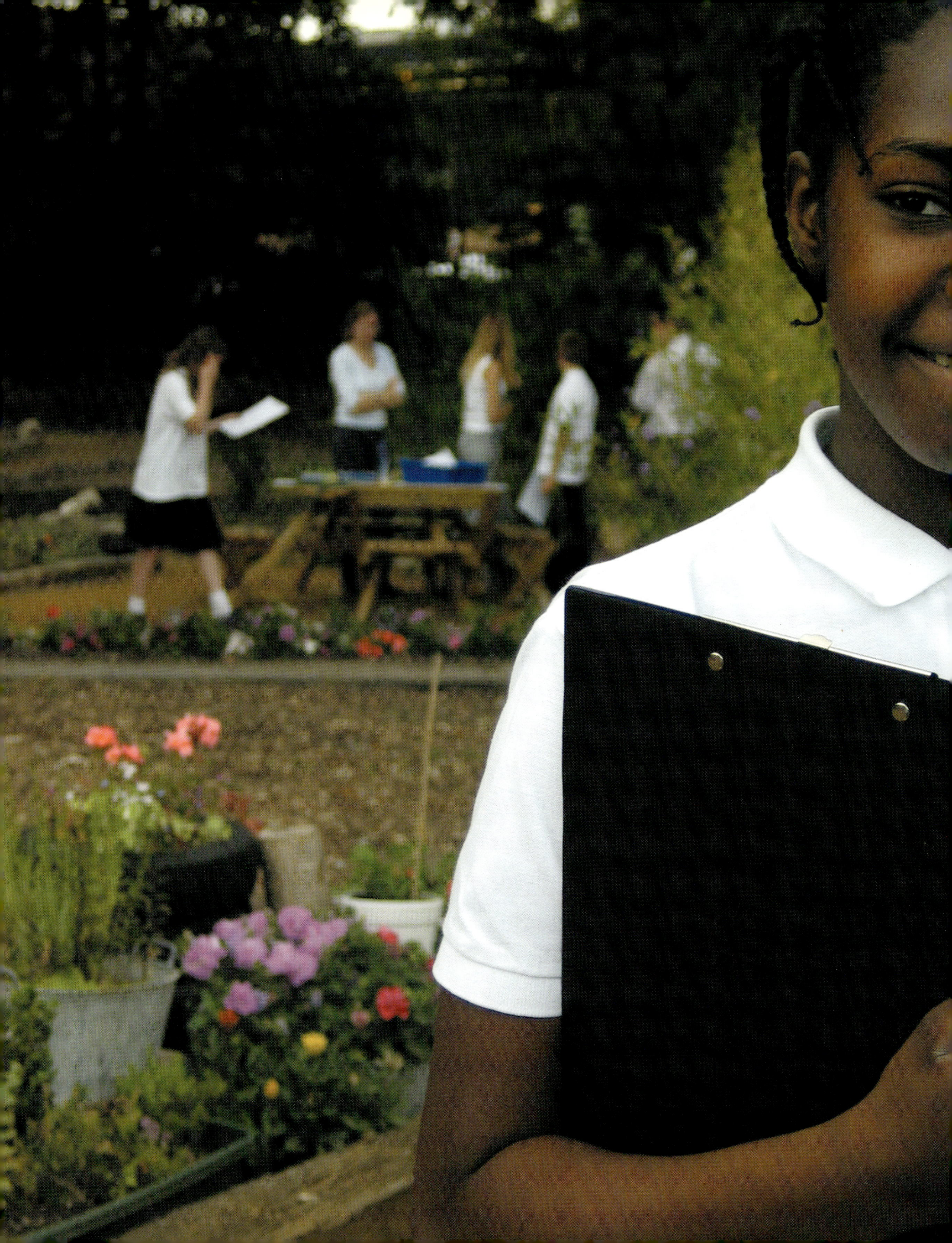

section **four**

**further
information**

Glossary of terms

Asset Management Plan (AMP)
The LEA's strategic assessment to identify the building work needed in schools to address deficiencies in condition, suitability and sufficiency. For guidance see
www.teachernet.gov.uk/amps

Biodiversity
Number and variety of living organisms; includes genetic diversity, species diversity, and ecological diversity.

Biodiversity Action Plan (BAP)
A plan that sets objectives and actions for the improvement and protection of biodiversity, with measurable targets. BAPs can be national, regional or local.

Brief
A brief is a structured document identifying and itemising the client's needs produced at key points in a project. This is a formal document. A strategic brief sets out the vision for the school's future and the needs and priorities of all the key stakeholders, to inform the overall masterplan of the school. A project brief sets out more detail for each project or phase of the overall plan.

Brownfield Site
Land previously developed for urban, industrial, military or infrastructure purposes or which has been damaged by previous use.

BS4428
British Standard Code of Practice for Landscape Operations (1989). There's further information at British Standards Online.
www.bsonline.bsi-global.com

BS5930
British Standard Code of Practice for Site Investigations (1999). Further information is at British Standards Online.
www.bsonline.bsi-global.com

BTEC
Business and Technology Education Council. Courses that develop a broad range of skills in job-related areas.

Building Bulletins
Priced publications, available from The Stationery Office, produced by the DfES to give design guidance for a wide variety of curriculum subjects, building issues and types of school provision. Some key bulletins are listed in **further reading**.

Building Schools for the Future (BSF)
A Government programme set up to deliver new and refurbished secondary schools over the next 15 years, using a mixture of PFI and conventional funding with private sector involvement.

Capital costs
The costs of acquiring or enhancing assets such as buildings, equipments or grounds. They can include the cost of site preparation and clearance, construction and installation, and professional fees.

Community Partnerships
Partnerships with community agencies which are used to identify genuine needs, provide mentorship, and contribute assets towards completing a project. In a successful partnership, all sides will give to, and benefit from, the project.

DfES
Department for Education and Skills.

DH
Department of Health.

Early years
Children between the ages of 0 and 5. Within this the Foundation Stage is the curriculum for children between the ages of 3 and 5. Early years settings in receipt of the 'nursery grant' follow the Foundation Stage Curriculum. The DfES guidance, *Birth to Three Matters*, addresses the development and education of very young children from birth to 3.

Easements
Voluntary agreements in which a property owner agrees to certain restrictions, protections, or activities. Easements are legally recognised, are generally held by a not-for-profit organisation, and may be established for an agreed-upon period of time or in perpetuity.

Eco-schools
An international programme which provides a simple framework enabling schools to analyse operations and become more sustainable. Pupil involvement is key, and the programme aims to help children become more effective citizens by encouraging them to take responsibility for the future of their own environment.
See www.eco-schools.org.uk or call ENCAMS on 01942 612621.

designing school grounds

Extended Schools
An extended school is one that provides a range of activities and services, often beyond the school day, to help meet the needs of its pupils, their families and the wider community. Across the country many schools are already providing extended services, which could for example include adult education, study support, ICT facilities and community sports programmes. See www.teachernet.gov.uk/extendedschools

Formal Curriculum
The National Curriculum and Foundation Stage requirements containing specific attainment targets and learning goals. The formal curriculum may be organised and delivered via discrete subject areas or through a cross-curricular approach.

Friendship stops, buddy benches and playground squads
Help to create a caring ethos within the grounds by providing places where pupils can go to find others to play or spend time with. Playground Squads are teams of pupils who help support adults on duty and pupils during breaktimes.

Greenfield Site
Land previously in agriculture or non-urban/industrial use or which has not been damaged by a previous use.

Hidden Curriculum
The semiotics of the school environment – how the place feels, what messages the place gives to those who use it.

Inactive edges
The blank walls of buildings where there are no windows, no doors, no activity going on, and limited or no casual surveillance from any overlooking windows.

Informal Curriculum
The learning and development opportunities available to children and young people outside of the formal curriculum delivery. Many of these opportunities occur at break times, lunchtime and before and after school.

Learning through Landscapes (LTL)
The national school grounds organisation providing training, resources and support to all those involved in the design, use and management of school grounds. LTL also develops programmes and undertakes research that advances understanding of related issues for all sectors. See www.ltl.org.uk or call 01962 845811.

Masterplan (see Strategy Plan)
A plan representing all ideas for future development on one site. This will be a visual representation and there may be written explanatory notes. Commonly used by planners and designers.

National Healthy Schools Standard
Funded by the DfES and DH, the National Healthy Schools Programme encourages schools to take a whole school approach to the health and well-being of its pupils and staff. Schools are assessed against a range of criteria aiming to achieve the National Healthy Schools Standard. See www.wiredforhealth.gov.uk

NVQ
National Vocational Qualification, awarded for competent performance in work-based activities.

Private Finance Initiative (PFI)
A system for providing capital assets for the provision of public services. Typically, the private sector designs, builds and maintains schools and associated capital assets and then operates those to sell services to the public sector ie the local authority or the school governors.

Public Private Partnership (PPP)
A variation of privatisation in which elements of a service previously run solely by the public sector (eg the local authority) are provided through a partnership between the Government and one or more private sector companies. Unlike a full privatisation scheme, in which the new venture is expected to function like any other private business, the Government continues to participate in some way.

Safe Routes to Schools
A national programme which encourages children to walk or cycle to school, by improving the safety of pedestrian and cycle routes. See www.saferoutestoschools.org.uk or call Sustrans on 0117 915 0100.

School Council
A democratically-elected group of students who represent their peers and enable pupils to become partners in their own education, making a positive contribution to the school environment and ethos. Further information from School Councils UK at www.schoolcouncils.org or call 0845 456 9428.

School Grounds Professionals/Practitioners
Individuals and organisations with appropriate knowledge and skills, and the capacity to support schools in the design, use and management of their grounds.

School Sports Coordinators
Part of a Government initiative designed to raise standards in schools through improved and coordinated delivery of PE and Sport. The coordinators work with School Sports Partnerships to bring together individual schools, and with the wider community, including local sports clubs.

School Travel Plan
A document produced by a school in conjunction with the local authority, encompassing all issues relevant to journeys to and from school, and including concerns about health and safety, and proposals for ways to make improvements. Grants are available from the DfES/DfT to help state schools fund measures identified within their Travel Plans. Details are available from local authority school travel advisers.

Secured by Design
UK Police initiative supporting the principles of 'designing-out crime' by use of effective crime prevention and security standards for a range of applications, including in schools. *Secured by Design* supports one of the Government's key planning objectives – the creation of secure, quality places where people want to live and work. See www.securedbydesign.com

Strategy Plan
An overall, spatial plan which sets out feasible and agreed proposals for buildings, spaces, movement and land use in a school. Also referred to as a master, concept or vision plan, a strategy plan for the school grounds allows for change and evolution of the outside spaces over time.

Sustainable Development
Development which meets the needs of the present without compromising the ability of future generations to meet their own needs.

14-19 Agenda
The Government strategy to reform learning for 14- to 19-year olds, including an increased emphasis on personalised learning, the quality of the vocational offer and learning about the world of work. The strategy was published in *14-19: Opportunity and Excellence* in 2003.

Text references and information sources

DfES publications available from www.teachernet.gov.uk/publications or call 0845 60 222 60

Foreword

1. *Education Outside the Classroom: 2005 House of Commons Education and Skills Committee report.* ISBN 0215021908

Introduction

2. *The Children Act 2004: Every Child Matters, Change for Children,* HM Government. www.everychildmatters.gov.uk

Developing school grounds – the process

3. DQI for Schools. www.dqi.org.uk/schools

4. Participation is actively promoted through Citizenship Education, Education for Sustainable Development, Agenda 21, *Every Child Matters* and the United Nations Convention on the Rights of the Child.

5. *Workout: Secondary School Grounds Toolkit*, Learning through Landscapes 2005. ISBN 1-872865-33-X

6. RIBA work stages. www.riba.org

7. *Transforming Schools: an inspirational guide to remodelling secondary schools*, DfES 2004. DfES ref 1140-2004

8. *DfES Schools for the Future: Inspirational Design for PE & Sport Spaces*, DfES 2005. DfES ref 2064-2005DOC-EN

Designing and building

9. *Sustainable schools – design primer, Design of sustainable schools – case studies*, due for publication 2006. www.teachernet.gov.uk/sustainabledesign

10. *Secured by Design.* www.securedbydesign.com

Designing and building for... learning and teaching

11. *DfES Manifesto for Education Outside the Classroom*, consultation launched Nov 2005, publication due autumn 2006. www.dfes.gov.uk/consultations

12. *National Curriculum: Key Stages 1 & 2* ISBN 0-11-370066-0; *Key Stages 3 & 4* ISBN 0-11-370067-9. Available online at www.nc.uk.net

13. QCA schemes of work. www.qca.org.uk/8992 www.standards.dfes.gov.uk/schemes3

14. *"...In the School Grounds"* series. Includes Arts, English, Geography, Mathematics, History, PSHE, PE, Science, available from Southgate publishers. www.southgatepublishers.co.uk

15. *Best Play – What Play Provision should do for children*, published by the National Playing Fields Association March 2000. ISBN 094608533

Designing and building for... healthy lifestyles

16. Health Education Authority 1998.

17. *National PE, School Sport and Club Links Strategy*, 2002. www.teachernet.gov.uk/pe

18. BS EN 1176 – *Playground Equipment – requirements for the design, manufacture and installation of playground equipment*, available from The Stationery Office www.tso.org.uk

19. BS EN 1177 – *Impact Absorbing Surfacing – specifies requirements for surfacing to be used in children's playgrounds and the methodology for its testing*, available from The Stationery Office www.tso.org.uk

20. *Growing Schools Programme*, Aims to support and encourage schools to think creatively about how they develop and use their school grounds as a teaching and learning resource to deliver the national curriculum. www.teachernet.gov.uk/growingschools

21. *Health and Safety at Work Act 1974*, available online at www.hse.gov.uk

See also:

Royal Society for the Prevention of Accidents. www.rospa.org.uk

National Playing Fields Association. www.npfa.org

National Healthy Schools. www.wiredforhealth.gov.uk

Eco-schools. www.eco-schools.org.uk

Designing and building for... positive behaviour

22 *Special Places; Special People – the hidden curriculum of school grounds*, Wendy Titman, Learning through Landscapes/WWF-UK 1994. ISBN 0-947613-48-X

23 *Learning from Past Mistakes*, research into school grounds design and its influence on student behaviour, Oxford Brookes University Post Graduate Advanced Certificate in Environmental Design and Crime Prevention 2004 Felicity Robinson, Landscapes Naturally.

Designing and building for... community use and development

Being involved in school design, CABE 2004, available free in Adobe Acrobat format from www.cabe.org.uk/publications

Building Learning Communities – Making it happen, The Community Schools Network 2000.

Extended Schools – providing opportunities and services for all, DfES 2005. www.teachernet.gov.uk/wholeschool/extendedschools/

DfES Schools for the Future: Designing schools for extended services, DfES 2006. ISBN 1-84478-739-7

Designing and building for... sustainable outcomes

24 Sustainable Development. www.sustainable-development.gov.uk

25 Local Biodiversity Action Plans. www.ukbap.org.uk

26 School Travel Plans, further information available from www.dft.gov.uk or via Local Authorities.

Safe Routes to Schools. www.saferoutestoschools.org.uk

Designing and building for... different sectors and needs

27 Curriculum guidance for the Foundation Stage, QCA 2000

28 *Exercising Muscles and Minds* by Marjorie Ouvry, National Children's Bureau 2003. ISBN 1-9047870-1-0

29 *Outdoor play in the early years: management and innovation* by Helen Bilton 1998. ISBN 1-853469-52-1

30 *Listening to young children: the Mosaic Approach* by Alison Clark and Peter Moss, National Children's Bureau 2001. ISBN 1-900990-62-8

See also:

Creating a Space to Grow, Learning through Landscapes, by Gail Ryder-Richardson 2005. ISBN 1-84312-304-5

Early Years Toolkit, Learning through Landscapes, publication due 2006.

Primary School Toolkit, Learning through Landscapes 2000. ISBN 1-872865-29-1

31 *Grounds for Improvement: Final Report into the Secondary Action Research Programme*, Mark Rickinson, National Foundation for Educational Research, and Learning through Landscapes October 2004. www.ltl.org.uk

Workout: Secondary School Grounds Toolkit, Learning through Landscapes 2005. ISBN 1-872865-33-X

32 *DfES Building Bulletin 77: Designing for Pupils with Special Educational Needs and Disabilities in Schools* (revised), due for publication 2006.

33 *Grounds for Sharing – A guide to developing special school sites*, Jane Stoneham 1996. ISBN 1-872865-23-2

Supporting school grounds development – who can help

Details of organisations offering help and support can be found within this section.

Funding

34 Neighbourhood Renewal Fund. www.neighbourhood.gov.uk

35 Department for Communities and Local Government (DCLG). www.dclg.gov.uk

36 Charity Commission for England and Wales. www.charity-commission.gov.uk

37 Annual Survey of Hours and Earnings from the Office of National Statistics. www.statistics.gov.uk

See also:

Directory of Social Change. www.dsc.org.uk

The Charities Aid Foundation. www.cafonline.org

The Charities Information Bureau. www.cibfunding.org.uk

Further reading

General

The following DfES Building Bulletins give good guidance on the generic processes and needs of school grounds design:

- *BB71 Outdoor Classroom* (1999)
  ISBN 0-11-271061-1

- *BB83 Schools Environmental Assessment Method*
  ISBN 0-11-270920-6

- *BB85 Schools Grounds: a Guide to Good Practice* (1997)
  ISBN 0-11-270990-7

- *BB87 Guidelines for Environmental Design of Schools* (2003)
  2nd edition available to download on www.teachernet.gov.uk/schoolbuildings

- *BB98 Briefing Framework for Secondary School Projects* (2004)
  ISBN 0-11-271152-9

- *BB99 Briefing Framework for Primary School Projects* (2006)

and relating to crime prevention in schools:

- *BB69 Crime Prevention in Schools: Specification, Installation and Maintenance of Intruder Alarm Systems*
  ISBN 0-11-270677-0

All Building Bulletins are available from The Stationery Office www.tso.org.uk

Statutory requirements

The Education (School Premises) Regulations 1999, Part V, section 24 (available from The Stationery Office), requires that a school shall provide playing fields for pupils who have attained the age of 8 years, other than a pupil referral unit. The minimum area of team game playing fields for schools is given in Schedule 2 of the regulations. Protection of school playing fields is covered by Section 77 of the School Standards & Framework Act 1998.

There are a number of additional publications related to the design, use and management of school grounds. For further information contact Learning through Landscapes or go to www.ltl.org.uk